BLACK&DECKER®

HOME IMPROVEMENT LIBRARY™

Bathroom Remodeling

Cy DeCosse Incorporated
Minnetonka, Minnesota

Contents

Copyright © 1993
Cy DeCosse Incorporated
5900 Green Oak Drive
Minnetonka, Minnesota 55343
1-800-328-3895
All rights reserved
Printed in U.S.A.

Also available from the publisher:
Everyday Home Repairs, Decorating With Paint & Wallcovering, Carpentry: Tools • Shelves • Walls • Doors, Kitchen Remodeling, Building Decks, Home Plumbing Projects & Repairs, Basic Wiring & Electrical Repairs, Workshop Tips & Techniques, Advanced Home Wiring, Carpentry: Remodeling. Landscape Design & Construction, Built-In Projects for the Home, Refinishing & Finishing Wood, Exterior Home Repairs & Improvements, Home Masonry Repairs & Projects

Library of Congress
Cataloging-in-Publication Data

Bathroom remodeling.
p. cm.— (Black & Decker home improvement library)
Includes index.
ISBN 0-86573-728-2 (hardcover).
ISBN 0-86573-729-0 (softcover).
1. Bathrooms —Remodeling—Amateurs' manuals.
I. Cy DeCosse Incorporated.
II. Series.
TH4816.3.B37B38 1993
643'.52—dc20   93-14916

CY DECOSSE INCORPORATED

A COWLES MAGAZINES COMPANY

Chairman/CEO: Bruce Barnet
Chairman Emeritus: Cy DeCosse
President/COO: Nino Tarantino
Executive V.P./Editor-in-Chief: William B. Jones

Created by: The Editors of Cy DeCosse Incorporated, in cooperation with Black & Decker.  is a trademark of the Black & Decker Corporation, and is used under license.

"Wire-Nut®" is a registered trademark of Ideal Industries, Inc.

NOTICE TO READERS

This book provides useful instructions, but we cannot anticipate all of your working conditions or the characteristics of your materials and tools. For safety, you should use caution, care, and good judgment when following the procedures described in this book. Consider your own skill level and the instructions and safety precautions associated with the various tools and materials shown. Neither the publisher nor Black & Decker® can assume responsibility for any damage to property or injury to persons as a result of misuse of the information provided.

The instructions in this book conform to "The Uniform Plumbing Code," "The National Electrical Code Reference Book," and "The Uniform Building Code" current at the time of its original publication. Consult your local Building Department for information on building permits, codes, and other laws as they apply to your project.

Managing Editor: Paul Currie
Project Manager: Carol Harvatin
Senior Art Director: Tim Himsel
Art Director: Dave Schelitzche
Senior Editor: Bryan Trandem
Editor & Lead Writer: Mark Johanson
Editor: Anne Price
Technical Production Editor: Jim Huntley
Assistant Technical Production Editor: Gary Sandin
Copy Editor: Janice Cauley
Contributing Editor: Dick Sternberg
Shop Supervisor: Phil Juntti
Set Builders: John Nadeau, Mike Shaw, Greg Wallace
Director of Development Planning & Production: Jim Bindas
Production Manager: Amelia Merz

Production Staff: Diane Dreon, Adam Esco, Joe Fahey, Mike Hehner, Jeff Hickman, Robert Powers, Mike Schauer, Kay Wethern, Nik Wogstad
Studio Manager: Cathleen Shannon
Assistant Studio Manager: Rena Tassone
Lead Photographer: Mike Parker
Photographers: Rebecca Hawthorne, Rex Irmen, John Lauenstein, William Lindner, Mark Macemon, Paul Najlis, Chuck Nields
Contributing Photographers:
© Gallop Studios, p.13; © Susan Gilmore, p.9; © Hedrich-Blessing Photography, Courtesy of Eljer Bathroom Sets, p.10, Designed by Childs, Dreyfus Group, p.7; © Jessie Walker Photography, p.8
Models: Steve Podraza, Paul Toft

Contributing Manufacturers: American Olean, General Marble Co., NuTone, Pearl Baths Inc., Price Pfister Inc., Trayco Inc.
Contributing Photography: American Olean, General Marble Co., Kohler Co., NKBA (National Kitchen & Bath Association), Pearl Baths Inc., Trayco Inc.

Printed on American paper by:
R. R. Donnelley & Sons Co.
99 98 97 96 / 5 4 3 2 1

Bathroom Remodeling

You step into your old shower stall, and notice that another tile has come loose. You kick the broken tile remnants into a corner, and turn on the water. As soon as the water temperature is just right, someone flushes the downstairs toilet and you leap back from the scalding water, pulling down the shower curtain in the process.

By taking on a few simple remodeling projects, your mornings can begin on a much more pleasant note. Replace the crumbling tile in your shower stall with a maintenance-free shower surround. Install a new shower faucet with an anti-scald pressure regulator. Add grab bars in your tub and shower area. Put in a new water-saver toilet, add more storage space, or give yourself a real treat, and replace your ordinary bathtub with a new whirlpool tub.

A bathroom remodeling project doesn't have to be complicated. It may be as simple as replacing a leaky faucet or installing decorative tile-board around your tub area. Or you may prefer to do a complete bathroom renovation—tearing out the existing materials down to bare studs and subfloor. Whether simple or complex, a remodeling project can transform an unattractive bathroom into a bright and functional living area.

Remodeling a bathroom can be expensive. The average cost of a full renovation, when you hire a contractor to do the work, is about the same as the cost of a small car. By doing part or all of the remodeling work yourself, you can save thousands of dollars.

Bathroom Remodeling contains helpful how-to information on a wide range of projects for all skill levels. Some of the projects, however, require basic knowledge of carpentry, plumbing and wiring techniques. You can hire a professional to handle portions of the job you do not wish to attempt, and still save a lot of money by doing the rest of the work yourself.

Create a bright, open feeling through good use of lighting. Installing several light sources will minimize shadows that can create hazards and make it difficult to shave or apply makeup. A shower light will make any shower stall more inviting.

Designing & Planning Your Bathroom

Because so many activities occur in such a small space, remodeling a bathroom requires a lot of thorough planning and design work.

Begin the planning process by assessing your current bathroom. Is there enough storage space? Does it have non-skid floor surfaces, grab bars, and GFCI electrical circuit protectors? Are there long waits to use the bathroom? Talk with family members to get their ideas, then decide which type of bathroom will best suit your needs. Refer to the model bathroom designs on pages 8 to 13 for general design ideas that match your specific needs. Make lists of fixtures and features you want, and look through bathroom design magazines for more ideas. It also is helpful to visit retail bathroom showrooms to get information on new bathroom products.

If you plan to make any structural, wiring, or plumbing changes, consult a building inspector early in the planning process to find out exactly what you must do to comply with Codes.

How-to books on subjects like wiring, plumbing, and remodeling help you develop skills that are useful in bathroom remodeling.

6

Tips for Designing a Bathroom

Make good use of space. Space-efficient fixtures give you the features you need, even in a small or oddly shaped bathroom. The guest bath above includes several space-saving fixtures: a triangular corner toilet, an angled shower stall, a shallow vanity and cabinets, and a tank-topper cabinet.

Provide storage. Design your bathroom so each family member has his or her own storage area, even if it is only one drawer in a vanity.

Make access easy. Install fixtures that make your bathroom easier to use and safer for children, and elderly or physically challenged individuals. The shower above is equipped with grab bars, a seat, and adjustable shower head.

Respect privacy. A feeling of privacy is critical to good bathroom design, especially in large family baths designed for use by more than one person at the same time. Short partition walls next to fixtures like toilets and whirlpools create visual separation that makes shared bathrooms more comfortable for everyone.

A double-bowl countertop and vanity help make this bathroom suitable for a large family. The separate shower and tub, extra towel rods, ample cabinet space, and plenty of open floor space create a bathroom that can be used by several people at the same time.

Model Bathroom Designs

The Large Family Bath

A busy, growing family requires a large bathroom that meets every family member's needs. Borrowing space from an adjacent room or closet is a good way to create the necessary space for a large family bath. Installing extra fixtures, like a double-bowl sink and separate shower and tub areas, lets your bathroom accommodate several users at the same time—a useful feature, especially if your home has no second bathroom.

Storage is important in a large family bath. Make sure there are enough shelves and drawers so all family members have their own storage areas. Add enough lighting fixtures to brighten the entire space evenly.

Floorplan

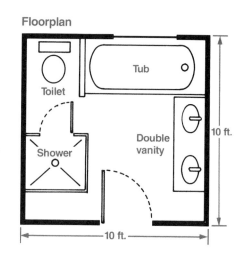

A combination tub-shower, equally useful for a quick morning shower or a relaxing evening soak, helps create a versatile family bath in a modest space. Custom cabinets designed to fit a unique wall area provide much-needed storage in this small bathroom. Extra-large mirrors make the room seem larger.

Model Bathroom Designs

The Small Family Bath

With careful design work and some creative planning, an average 5 ft. × 8 ft. bathroom can be remodeled to meet the diverse needs of a family.

Because it receives frequent use by all members of the family, a small family bath depends on versatile, space-efficient fixtures and storage cabinets. Space-saving features, like a combination tub-shower, and a recessed medicine cabinet, are common features in a small family bath. All family bathrooms receive heavy use, so using low-maintenance materials, like ceramic tile and enameled fixtures, can help you reduce cleaning chores.

Floorplan

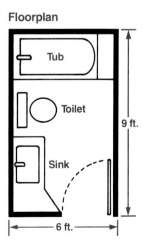

Visual appeal is as important as function in the luxury bath. This room uses custom ceramic tile, decorative brass faucets, and designer plumbing fixtures to create a showcase bathroom. The whirlpool tub is suitable for relaxed bathing by one or two people, and mood lighting and ornamental mirrors add a luxurious touch.

Model Bathroom Designs
The Luxury Bath

Luxury bathrooms that contain a whirlpool tub and designer fixtures are increasingly common, even in moderately priced homes. A luxury bathroom still requires a relatively large space, but many manufacturers now offer smaller luxury fixtures that are easy for the do-it-yourselfer to install. Custom cabinets, fine ceramic tile for the floor and walls, and decorative, upscale accessories can provide a feeling of luxury, even in smaller bathrooms.

Because relaxation is the goal of most luxury baths, the center-piece of the room usually is a whirlpool tub. Designers of luxury bathrooms often build on the "spa" environment created by a whirlpool by adding a sauna or exercise equipment.

Floorplan

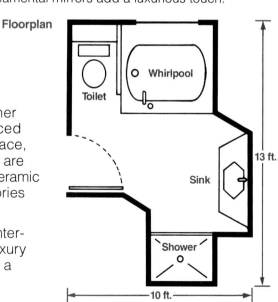

A whirlpool with door and built-in seat provides easy access for people with limited mobility. When the whirlpool is filled, the water pressure activates a door sealing mechanism that prevents leaks. Other elements of this barrier-free bathroom include a barrier-free sink, and safety grab bars around the toilet, shower, and tub.

Model Bathroom Designs

The Barrier-free Bath

A bathroom used frequently by an elderly family member, or by an individual who is physically challenged, has special requirements.

To protect against injuries, install cushioned vinyl flooring, and mount grab bars around the tub and toilet. Make sure the bathroom has adequate ventilation to prevent condensation that can make surfaces slippery. Choose cabinets, sinks, and other fixtures that have smooth, rounded edges, not sharp corners. Install bright lights to improve safety, and mount light switches and receptacles at lower heights, where they are more easily reached. Design the bathroom layout to include a clear turn around area that is at least 48" wide.

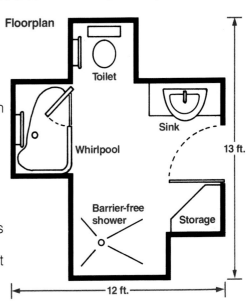

Floorplan

Toilet

Sink

Whirlpool

13 ft.

Barrier-free shower

Storage

12 ft.

A shower stall, here made of glass block, is a common feature of the guest bath, which does not need a bathtub. A pedestal sink is a good choice for a guest bath, since little storage room is needed.

Model Bathroom Designs

The Guest Bath

A guest bath usually is smaller than a family bath, but it should feature most of the same conveniences. In a guest bath, however, a separate shower stall can be substituted for the bathtub.

Keep decor in the guest bath simple, and make sure to provide sufficient lighting. The layout and the decor in a guest bathroom should create an open, airy feeling that welcomes your overnight visitors.

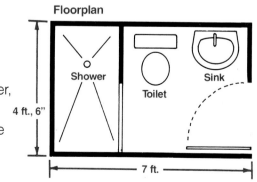

Floorplan

Shower

Toilet

Sink

4 ft., 6"

7 ft.

A pedestal sink is ideal for a half-bath because it is decorative, but does not take up much space. Natural wood flooring and wall paneling work well in a half-bath, where there is no tub or shower to cause moisture problems.

Model Bathroom Designs
The Half-Bath

The half-bath is a bathroom that contains a sink and toilet, but no shower or bathtub. Commonly installed on the first floor near entertainment areas, the half-bath should be designed with the comfort of visitors in mind. When decorating a half-bath, select neutral patterns and light colors that make small spaces seem larger.

Because floorspace is limited, install a pedestal sink and a simple wall mirror instead of a bulky vanity and wall cabinet.

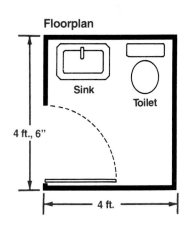

Floorplan

Sink

Toilet

4 ft., 6"

4 ft.

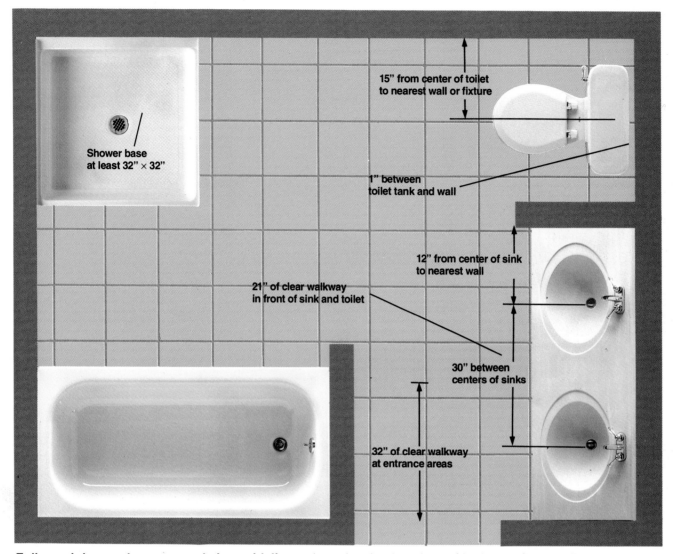

Shower base at least 32" × 32"

15" from center of toilet to nearest wall or fixture

1" between toilet tank and wall

12" from center of sink to nearest wall

21" of clear walkway in front of sink and toilet

30" between centers of sinks

32" of clear walkway at entrance areas

Follow minimum clearance and size guidelines when planning locations of bathroom fixtures. Easy access to fixtures is fundamental to creating a bathroom that is comfortable, safe, and easy to use.

Making a Bathroom Remodeling Plan

After you have reached a decision about the type of bathroom you want, make a specific and thorough bathroom plan.

You will need to make drawings and a materials list, set budgets and timetables, and decide when to do the work yourself, and when to hire help. You also may need to obtain a building permit and make arrangements to have your work inspected.

To simplify your remodeling project, use existing plumbing and wiring wherever possible. Major bathroom renovations can be accomplished without relocating the main bathroom fixtures (see pages 20 to 21). Moving a drain pipe for a

toilet, in particular, is difficult to do yourself, and very expensive if you decide to hire a plumber for the job.

If you plan to remove part or all of a wall to expand your bathroom, determine whether the wall is load-bearing before you cut any wall studs. If you are unsure about the special support requirements of load-bearing walls, contact your building inspector. Make sure your entire project conforms with all of your local Building Codes (see page 15).

If you have only one bathroom in your home, arrange for alternate accommodations while your remodeling project is underway.

Options for Remodeling Projects

A full remodeling project involves removing old wall and floor surfaces down to bare studs and subfloor, then replacing major bathroom fixtures, and wall and floor surfaces. A full remodeling project creates a dramatic new bathroom that will serve your family's needs for many years to come. Replacing all of your major bathroom fixtures and your floor and wall surfaces at the same time is the most efficient way to remodel your bathroom.

A bathroom update can be as simple as replacing an out-of-date or unattractive sink faucet, or installing a new medicine cabinet and light fixture. A few well-selected updates done in a weekend or two can transform a plain bathroom into a pleasant, inviting part of your home.

Checklist for Bathroom Planning & Design

All of the following recommendations meet or exceed national and most local Building Codes. Always check with your local building inspector for specific codes in your area.

❏ Include a vent fan (pages 116 to 119), even if your bathroom has natural ventilation

❏ Install adequate lighting (pages 114 to 115)

❏ Install a ground-fault circuit interrupter (GFCI) on all receptacles (page 114), and wire all bathroom circuits through the GFCI

❏ Do not install a light switch within 60" of any bathtub or shower (page 17)

❏ All light fixtures above showers and tubs must be vaporproof

❏ Maintain a distance of at least 6" between major bathroom fixtures

❏ Bathtub faucets should be accessible from outside of the tub (pages 108 to 109)

❏ Install at least one grab bar at the entrance to a tub or shower (page 121)

❏ Avoid building whirlpool decks that require more than one step. Steps should be at least 10" deep, and no higher than 7¼" (page 17)

❏ Install a shower seat (page 7)

❏ Shower door must swing out, away from the shower (pages 16 and 122)

❏ Add an anti-scald device to showers to protect against burns (page 62)

❏ Use non-slip flooring material (page 80)

❏ Include storage around sink for personal grooming supplies (pages 98 to 99)

❏ Include storage in shower-tub area for personal care products (page 62)

❏ Install towel rods or rings, and hooks for clothing or towels (pages 120 to 121)

Tips for Bathroom Planning

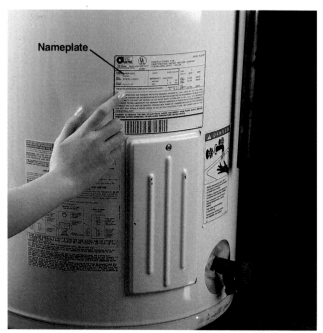

Borrow space from an adjacent room or an under-used closet to expand your bathroom. A few additional square feet of functional floor space greatly increases your number of remodeling possibilities.

Check your water heater to make sure it has enough capacity to support additional fixtures, like a whirlpool or a second shower. A family of four with two bathrooms should have at least a 50-gallon water heater, but a couple with one bathroom needs only a 30-gallon unit. The capacity of a water heater is listed on the nameplate.

Replace a large window in a tub area with a smaller window, especially when adding a tub surround and shower. An awning window (above) provides as much ventilation as the larger, double-hung window that it replaced. Smaller replacement windows require some patching of exterior wall surfaces. Check wall studs and window framing for water damage.

Build your own cabinets and countertops to give your bathroom unique character. A custom countertop like the one pictured above is easy to make and can be used to fit an unusual space or to replace an old vanity top on a custom cabinet. Sheet laminates (above) are water-resistant and relatively easy to work with for most do-it-yourselfers.

Keep whirlpool decks low. If a step is needed, build it at least 10" deep, and no more than 7¼" in height. If the height of your whirlpool requires more than one step, most Local Codes require that you install a hand railing.

Keep water and electricity apart. Do not install light switches within 60" of tubs or showers. All receptacles in bathrooms should be GFCI-protected to guard against electric shocks.

Make a materials list and budget to help keep your expenses under control. Include accessories and other items that are purchased separately, like sink faucets and vanity countertops. If you are hiring a contractor to do any of the work, remember to include his or her fee in the budget.

Draw a floorplan of your new bathroom. The plan should include distances between fixtures, wiring and plumbing details, and an elevation drawing that shows heights of all fixtures and accessories. If you are not planning any structural, wiring, or plumbing changes, you need only make a scaled sketch of the bathroom to make sure new fixtures will fit.

Tools & Materials for Bathroom Remodeling

Get the right tools for the job before you begin. In addition to the basic tools required for most remodeling projects (see list below), a number of specialty tools that simplify a bathroom remodeling project are available. Among them are tools for working with wiring, plumbing, and ceramic tile.

Whenever you are using a tool for the first time, practice on scrap materials before doing the actual work.

Because bathrooms usually are small (less than 50 square feet), purchasing cheap building materials will not save you much on your initial cost. Spending a little more for quality building materials will increase your enjoyment of your new bathroom, and make it last longer.

Basic Tools for Remodeling

- Adjustable wrench
- Ratchet wrench
- Hammer
- Masonry hammer
- Wood chisel
- Masonry chisel
- Putty knife
- Notched trowel
- Wallboard knife
- Flat pry bar
- Wrecking bar
- Hacksaw
- Screwdrivers
- Tape measure
- Marker
- Staple gun
- Clamps
- Sponge
- Paint brush
- Cable ripper
- Neon circuit tester
- Carpenter's level

Specialty Tools for Bathroom Remodeling

Wire stripper

Tile cutter

Rod saw

Power Tools for Bathroom Remodeling

Cordless drill

Hole saw

Jig saw

Cordless screwdriver

Circular saw

Reciprocating saw

Heat gun

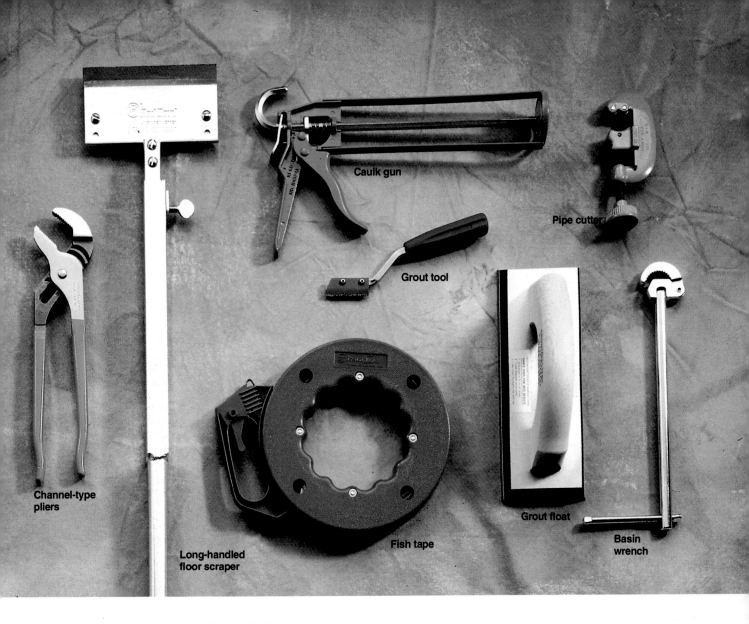

Channel-type pliers

Caulk gun

Pipe cutter

Grout tool

Basin wrench

Long-handled floor scraper

Fish tape

Grout float

Materials for Bathroom Remodeling

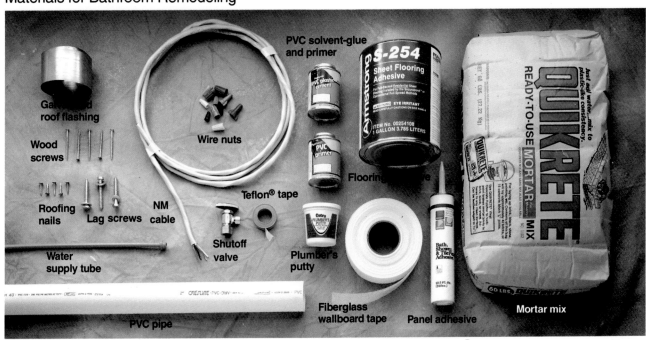

Galvanized roof flashing

Wood screws

Roofing nails

Lag screws

NM cable

Water supply tube

PVC pipe

Wire nuts

Shutoff valve

Teflon® tape

Plumber's putty

Fiberglass wallboard tape

Panel adhesive

PVC solvent-glue and primer

PVC plastic cement

PVC primer

Flooring adhesive

Mortar mix

Bathroom Remodeling: A Step-by-step Overview

Most major bathroom remodeling projects should follow the same basic steps. Take out smaller and more easily removed fixtures, like sinks and toilets, first. Next, remove wall and floor surfaces. Completing these projects first simplifies the more difficult task of removing bathtubs and showers. Inspect framing and repair any structural damage, then complete new framing and rough-in work. Finally, install new bathroom fixtures and surfaces in reverse order from removal.

1 Remove old toilet, sink, cabinets, electrical fixtures, and accessories (pages 24 to 37).

2 Remove wall and floor surfaces down to the bare studs and subfloor (pages 38 to 41).

3 Remove bathtubs and shower stalls (pages 32 to 35), then examine wall and floor structure for signs of damage (pages 39 and 95).

4 Make any structural repairs that are needed, then do the rough plumbing, wiring, and framing work (pages 42 to 55).

5 Install new bathtubs, showers, and whirlpools (pages 58 to 79).

6 Install new wall surfaces and wall coverings, replace flooring underlayment, then install new floor coverings (pages 80 to 97).

7 Install cabinets, countertop, sink, and remaining plumbing fixtures (pages 98 to 113).

8 Connect vent fan and electrical fixtures, then install accessories. Caulk around all fixtures and at the joints between the floor and the walls (pages 114 to 124).

Bathroom Remodeling Basics

Removing Bathroom Fixtures & Surfaces

Do removal work quickly and easily by using the right tools for the job. A reciprocating saw with a combination blade cuts through old mortar and tile grout, turning a time-consuming chore into a simple job.

Begin the removal phase of your project by removing fixtures located near the door, such as the toilet and sink. Even if you plan to keep these fixtures, get them out of the way so they are not damaged, and to clear the way for removing other fixtures. Also take out cabinets, vanities, electrical fixtures, and bathroom accessories.

Remove old bathtubs and shower stalls only after you have created a clear path to get them out. That may mean removing trim and the wall and floor coverings first. Label trim and other items you plan to reuse, then store them in an out-of-the-way spot. Plan to get help removing heavy fixtures, like a bathtub.

Turn off water supply and electrical power to the bathroom before removing electrical and plumbing fixtures, or cutting into walls or ceilings.

This section shows:

- Removing toilets (pages 26 to 27)
- Removing sinks, countertops & cabinets (pages 28 to 31)
- Removing bathtubs & showers (pages 32 to 35)
- Removing electrical fixtures & bathroom accessories (pages 36 to 37)
- Removing wall & floor surfaces (pages 38 to 41)

Tips for Removing Bathroom Fixtures

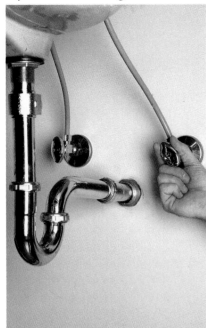

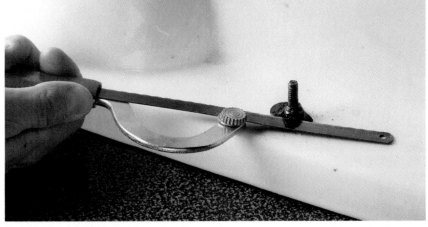

Cut corroded bolts with a hacksaw if you cannot loosen the nut with a wrench and you wish to remove the old fixture intact. Often, floor bolts on toilet bowls, like the one above, must be sawed off.

Turn off shutoff valves, mounted near fixtures on the water supply lines, before disconnecting water pipes. Sinks and toilets usually are equipped with easily accessible shutoff valves, but many bathtubs and showers are not.

Crack corroded nuts with a nut splitter if you cannot reach the bolt with a hacksaw or wrench. Bolts that connect toilet tanks and bowls (above) and coupling nuts that connect faucets to supply lines can be difficult to reach. Nut splitters are sold at most automobile parts stores.

Turn off the main shutoff valve when there are no individual shutoff valves at the fixture being removed. Main shutoff valves usually are located in your basement, near the water meter.

Plug drain pipes with a rag or a pipe cap if they will be open for more than a few minutes. Uncovered waste pipes allow dangerous sewer gases to escape into your home.

Removing Toilets

The toilet is the first fixture to be removed in most remodeling projects. Loosening corroded or rusted nuts and bolts is the most difficult part of the process. See page 25 for tips on removing problem nuts.

Old toilets that will not be reinstalled may be broken up into small, easily managed pieces with a sledgehammer. Disconnect the toilet and cover it with a heavy blanket before breaking it. Wear eye protection, long sleeves, and work gloves when handling the fragments.

> **Everything You Need:**
>
> Tools: adjustable wrench, ratchet wrench and sockets, putty knife, basin wrench.
>
> Materials: rag, bucket.

Most toilets are fragile and should be removed during full remodeling projects, even if you do not plan to replace them. Always use care when handling any fixture made of china or porcelain.

Tips for Removing Toilets

Protect your floor with a tarp when removing the toilet, if you plan to keep the original floor covering. Residue from the wax ring seal between the bottom of the toilet and the toilet flange is very difficult to remove from floor coverings.

Disconnect any pipes between a wall-mounted toilet tank and the bowl, after turning off the water supply and emptying the tank. Older toilets, like the one shown above, often have a metal elbow that connects the tank to the bowl. Set 2 x 4 braces below the tank before detaching it from the wall.

How to Remove a Toilet

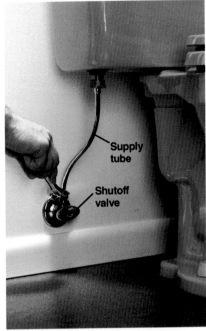

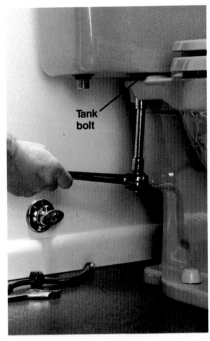

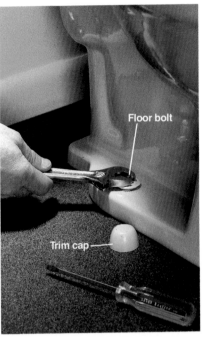

1 Turn off the shutoff valve on the water supply line, then flush the toilet to empty the tank and bowl. Sponge tank and bowl dry, then disconnect the water supply tube at the shutoff valve and the bottom of the toilet tank.

2 Remove the nuts from the tank bolts with a ratchet wrench or basin wrench (see page 25 for tips on removing problem nuts). Carefully lift the tank off the bowl, and set it aside.

3 Pry off the trim caps from the floor bolts, then remove the nuts from the floor bolts, using an adjustable wrench.

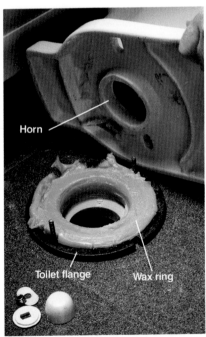

4 Straddle the toilet bowl and rock it gently until it breaks loose from the wax seal between the toilet horn and the toilet flange. Lift the bowl up, then lay it on its side near the work area.

5 Remove the old wax seal from the toilet flange and horn, using a putty knife. Clean the flange and the horn with a stiff wire brush, then disinfect the flange with a strong bleach solution.

6 Stuff a rag into the drain opening to keep sewer gas from escaping. Protect the flange with an inverted pail until you are ready to install the new toilet.

Removing Sinks, Cabinets & Countertops

Replacing bathroom sinks, countertops, and cabinets is a quick and relatively inexpensive way to give your bathroom a fresh, new look.

Disconnect plumbing first, then remove the sink basin or integral sink-countertop unit. Next, take out any remaining countertops. Finally, remove cabinets and vanities.

Everything You Need:

Tools: channel-type pliers, adjustable wrench, basin wrench, reciprocating saw, screwdriver, utility knife, flat pry bar.

Cut apart cabinets and vanities to simplify removal and disposal. A reciprocating saw or jig saw works well for this job.

How to Disconnect a Sink

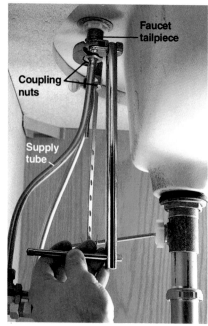

1 Turn off the shutoff valves, then remove the coupling nuts that connect the supply tube to the faucet tailpieces, using a basin wrench. If supply tubes are soldered, cut them above the shutoff valves.

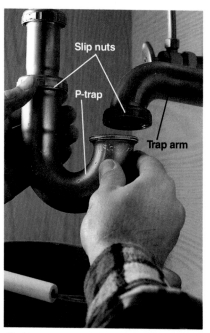

2 With bucket beneath, remove P-trap by loosening slip nuts at both ends. If the nuts will not turn, cut out the drain trap with a hacksaw. When prying or cutting, take care to avoid damaging the trap arm that runs into the wall.

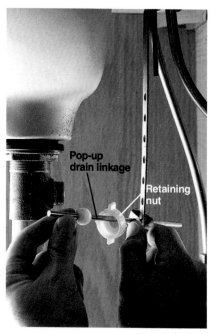

Sink with faucet mounted on the countertop: Disconnect pop-up drain linkage from the tailpiece of the sink drain by unscrewing the retaining nut.

How to Remove a Sink

Shown in cross-section for clarity

Mounting clip

Self-rimming sink: Disconnect plumbing, then slice through any caulking or sealant between the sink rim and the countertop, using a utility knife. Lift the sink off the countertop.

Rimless sink: Disconnect plumbing, including the drain tailpiece. To support the sink, tie wire around a piece of scrap wood and set the wood across the sink opening. Thread the wire down through the drain hole and attach it to another scrap of wood. Twist wire until taut, then detach mounting clips. Slice caulking, slowly loosen wire, and remove sink.

Wall-mounted sink: Disconnect plumbing, slice through any caulk or sealant, then lift sink off wall brackets. Some models are attached to the wall with lag screws. For this type, wedge 2 × 4s between the sink and floor to support it while screws are removed.

Pedestal sink: Disconnect the plumbing. If sink and pedestal are bolted together, disconnect them. Remove the pedestal first, supporting the sink from below with 2 × 4s. Lift the sink off the wall brackets (photo, left).

Integral sink-countertop: Disconnect plumbing, then detach mounting hardware underneath the countertop. Slice through caulk or sealant between countertop and wall and between countertop and vanity, then lift the sink-countertop unit off the vanity.

How to Remove a Wall Cabinet

1 Remove cabinet doors and mirrors, if possible. If cabinet has electrical features, see variation shown below.

2 Remove screws or any other anchors that hold the sides of the cabinet to the wall studs.

3 Pull the cabinet out of the wall cavity. Pry the cabinet loose with a pry bar, or grip the face frame of the cabinet with pliers to pull it out.

Variations for Wall-mounted Cabinets

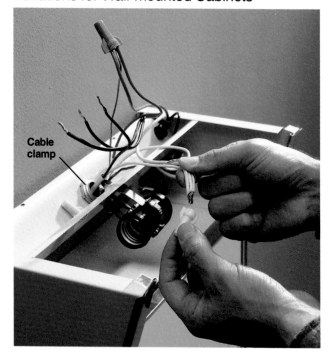

Cable clamp

Cabinets with built-in electrical features: Shut off power, then disconnect built-in lights or receptacles (see pages 36 to 37). Unscrew the cable clamp on the back of the connection box so cable is loose when the cabinet is removed.

Surface-mounted cabinets: Support the cabinet body from below with 2 × 4 braces, then remove the mounting screws to free the cabinet from the wall. When removing a large cabinet, have a helper hold the cabinet while you work.

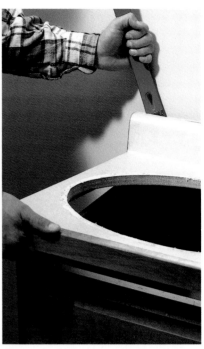

1 Disconnect plumbing (page 28), then cut through any caulk or sealant between the backsplash and the wall.

2 Detach any mounting hardware, located underneath the countertop inside the vanity.

3 Remove the countertop from the vanity, using a pry bar if necessary.

Cabinets with solid backs: Turn off the main water supply, then remove shutoff valves, preserving as much of the supply pipe as possible. Cap supply pipes or install new shutoff valves after the vanity is removed, then turn water supply back on.

4 Remove the screws or nails (usually driven through the back rail of the cabinet) that anchor the vanity to the wall.

5 Cut through any caulk or sealant between the vanity and wall, using a utility knife, then pry the vanity away from the wall.

Shower
pipe
Faucet
body

Shutoff
valves

Supply
pipes

Removing Bathtubs & Showers

Bathtubs and showers are heavy and bulky fixtures, so they pose special problems for removal. Unless the tub or shower has unique salvage value, cut or break the unit into pieces for easy removal and disposal. This technique allows one person to handle most of the disposal chores. Always wear eye protection and gloves when cutting or breaking apart fixtures.

For most tubs and showers, you need to remove at least 6" of wall surface around the tub to gain access to fasteners holding it to the wall studs. Maneuvering a tub out of an alcove also is easier when the wall surfaces are removed. If you are replacing the entire wall surface, do all the demolition work before removing the tub.

Disconnect the faucet through the access panel, usually located on the wall surface behind or next to the tub faucet and drain. (If tub does not have an access panel, add one as directed on page 81.) Turn off the shutoff valves, then cut the shower pipe above the faucet body. Disconnect or cut off supply pipes above the shutoff valves.

Everything You Need:

Tools: reciprocating saw, channel-type pliers, screwdriver, hacksaw, adjustable wrench, flat pry bar, wrecking bar, metal snips.

Materials: 2 × 4 or 1 × 4 lumber.

How to Remove Handles & Spouts

1 Shut off the water supply, then remove the faucet handles by prying off covers and unscrewing the mounting screws.

2 Remove tub spout by inserting a screwdriver into the spout and twisting counterclockwise until it unscrews from the stub-out that extends from wall plumbing.

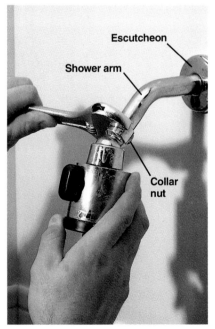

Escutcheon

Shower arm

Collar
nut

3 Unscrew the collar nut to remove shower head. Loosen the escutcheon plate, then twist the shower arm counterclockwise to unscrew it from wall plumbing.

How to Remove a Bathtub Drain

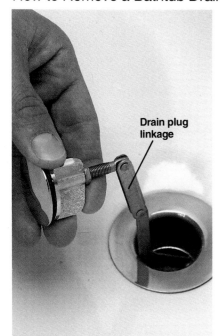

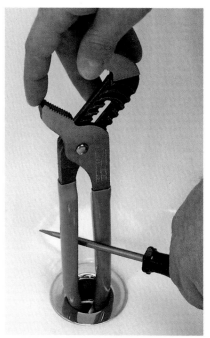

1 Remove the drain plug. Most bathtub plugs are connected to drain plug linkage that is lifted out along with the plug.

Spring-mounted drain plugs: Remove the plug by unscrewing it from the drain crosspiece.

2 Disconnect the drain assembly from the tub by inserting a pair of pliers into the drain opening and turning the crosspiece counter-clockwise. Insert a long screwdriver between the handles and use it to twist the pliers.

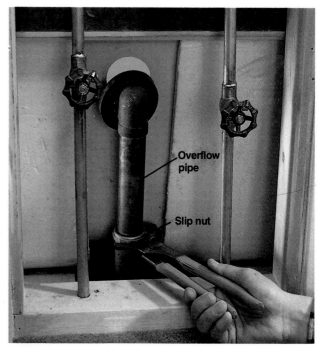

3 Remove the screws in the overflow coverplate (top photo). Remove the coverplate along with any attached drain plug linkage (bottom photo).

4 Remove the overflow pipe by unscrewing the slip nut that holds it to the rest of the drain assembly, then lifting out the pipe. Stuff a rag into the waste pipe after the overflow pipe is removed to keep sewer gases from entering your home.

33

How to Remove a Shower Stall

1 After disconnecting faucet handles, spout and shower head (page 32), remove the shower curtain rod or shower door, molding or trim, and any other accessories.

2 Slice the caulking around each shower panel, using a utility knife. Remove any screws holding panels together. NOTE: Custom-tiled shower stall walls are removed in the same way as any ceramic tile wall (see page 40).

3 Pry panels away from the wall, using a flat pry bar. If panels are still intact, cut them into small pieces for easier disposal, using a jig saw or a sharp utility knife.

Fabricated shower base (fiberglass or plastic): Slice the caulking between the base and the floor, then unscrew any fasteners holding the base to the wall studs. Pry the base from the floor with a wrecking bar.

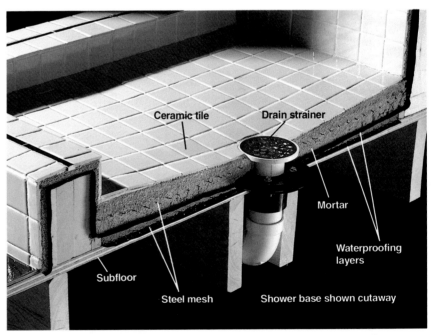

Ceramic tile

Drain strainer

Mortar

Waterproofing layers

Subfloor

Steel mesh

Shower base shown cutaway

Ceramic-tile shower base: Remove the drain strainer, then stuff a rag into the drain opening. Wearing protective equipment, break apart a section of tile with a hammer and masonry chisel. Cut through any steel mesh reinforcement, using a metal snips. Continue knocking tile and mortar loose until the waterproofing layers are exposed, then scrape off the layers with a long-handled floor scraper (see page 40).

How to Remove a Bathtub

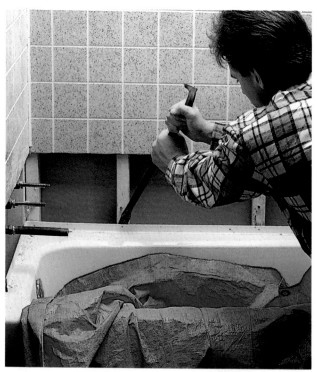

1 Use a reciprocating saw to cut away at least 6" of the wall surface above the tub on all sides. Before cutting, be sure faucet handles, spout, and drain are disconnected (pages 32 to 33).

2 Remove fasteners that hold the tub flanges to the wall studs, then use a wrecking bar or a piece of 2 × 4 to pry the bathtub loose.

3 Lift the edge of the bathtub, and slip a pair of soaped 1 × 4 runners beneath the tub apron. Pull the tub away from the wall, using the runners as skids. Use helpers when removing steel and cast-iron tubs.

4 Cut or break the bathtub into small pieces for easy disposal. Fiberglass, reinforced polymer, or pressed steel tubs can be cut with a reciprocating saw, but cast-iron tubs should be covered with a heavy tarp and broken apart with a sledgehammer.

Removing Electrical Fixtures & Bathroom Accessories

Electrical fixtures and bathroom accessories should be disconnected and removed in the order that best suits your own remodeling project.

Remove fragile accessories, like porcelain towel rods and vanity lights, early in the project so they are not damaged, but leave electrical receptacles and light fixtures in place as long as possible to provide light and power for tools. Store accessories in a safe place if you are planning to reinstall them.

Everything You Need:

Tools: screwdrivers, neon circuit tester.

Materials: rags, wire nuts, duct tape.

Remove shower lights and other fixtures before removing wall and ceiling surfaces. If you plan to reinstall the shower light, take care not to lose or damage the waterproof gasket that fits between the light cover and the ceiling. Remove the metal canister for recessed light fixtures after the wiring is disconnected and the ceiling surface is removed.

Tips for Removing Accessories

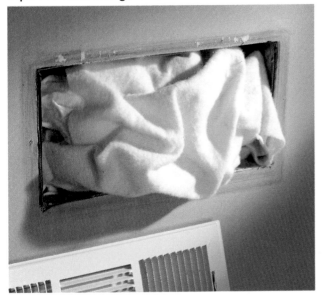

Remove coverplates from ductwork and vent fan units, then stuff them with rags to keep debris and dust from circulating.

Unscrew the mounting plates holding surface-mounted towel rods, toilet paper holders, and other bathroom accessories.

How to Remove Electrical Fixtures

1 Shut off electrical power to the bathroom circuits at the main service panel.

2 Loosen mounting screws, then remove the bases and coverplates from lights and other electrical fixtures. Be careful not to touch wires until they have been tested for power.

3 Test circuit wires for power, using a neon circuit tester. Touch one probe to a grounding screw, and the other to each circuit wire connection. If the circuit tester light glows, turn off the main circuit breaker, and retest.

4 When you are sure power is off, disconnect the fixture or receptacle from the circuit wires.

5 Use wire nuts to cap bare wire ends. If more than one circuit cable enters the electrical box, group wires by color, and cap wires of the same color together.

6 Cover the electrical box with duct tape to keep out dust and debris during demolition.

Remove old wall surfaces in small sections, using a reciprocating saw. Cutting ceramic tile walls into sections is easier than chipping away individual tiles. For general safety, shut off electrical power and water supply lines, and check for pipes and wires before cutting into any wall.

Damaged framing members may be concealed by water-damaged wall or floor surfaces. If any portion of wall surface shows peeling, discoloration, or bowing, remove the entire surface to examine the framing members. Repair or reinforce damaged framing members before installing new wall surfaces.

Removing Wall & Floor Surfaces

Removing and replacing wall and floor surfaces has two main benefits. First, the access to wall cavities makes it much easier to update or expand bathroom plumbing and electrical systems. Second, removing surfaces lets you check the framing members behind walls and under floors for water damage and warping.

Do not try to install a new wall surface, such as ceramic tile, over old plaster or wallboard. This practice may seem to save time, but by concealing possible structural problems inside the walls, it actually may create more work in the long run.

Everything You Need:

Tools: reciprocating saw, long-handled floor scraper, pry bar, masonry chisel, masonry hammer, heat gun, putty knives, utility knife.

Materials: trisodium phosphate (TSP).

Tips for Removing Wall & Floor Surfaces

Inspect walls and floors for signs of warping or water damage before you remove the surfaces. Drag a long straightedge across the floor or wall to help detect valleys and bulges in the surface, which indicate that your wall or floor may have structural problems (see pages 44 and 45 for repair tips).

Pry off trim and molding. Loosen long pieces of trim a little at a time to prevent splintering. Use blocking between the pry bar and the wall to increase leverage. Label trim pieces as they are removed so you can reattach them properly.

Wear protective equipment when removing old wall and floor surfaces. Protective equipment should include a particle mask, eye protection, hearing protection, long-sleeved shirt, gloves, and sturdy shoes.

Use a masonry chisel and masonry hammer to chip away ceramic floor tile. Chipping away tiles makes it easier to cut the mortar bed and any underlayment into small sections for removal (page 40).

How to Remove Ceramic Wall Tile

1 Knock a small starter hole in the bottom of the wall, using a masonry hammer and masonry chisel. Be sure the floor is covered with a heavy tarp, and electricity and water are shut off.

2 Begin cutting out small sections of wall by inserting a reciprocating saw with a bimetal blade into the hole, and cutting along grout lines. Be careful when sawing near pipes and wiring.

3 Cut the entire wall surface into small sections, removing each section as it is cut.

How to Remove Ceramic Floor Tile

Ceramic tile set in adhesive: Chip away tile, using a masonry hammer and masonry chisel, then use a long-handled floor scraper to scrape away tile fragments and old adhesive residue. A floor sander may be used to create a smooth finish on the subfloor.

Ceramic tile set in mortar: Chip away tile, using a masonry hammer and chisel. Cut the old subfloor into small sections, using a circular saw with an old carbide blade. Pry up individual sections of floor with a wrecking bar. NOTE: If the old tile was laid on underlayment, raise the blade of the saw so it cuts through underlayment and mortar, but not subfloor.

How to Remove Vinyl Floor Tiles

1 Soften flooring adhesive by warming tiles with a heat gun. Wear eye protection and gloves.

2 Pry up tiles with a putty knife or a wallboard knife, then use the knife to scrape old adhesive residue off the underlayment or the subfloor.

3 Remove stubborn tile adhesive with a long-handled floor scraper.

How to Remove Sheet-vinyl Flooring

1 Remove baseboards, then cut the old flooring into 10"-wide strips, using a utility knife or a flooring knife. Cut through both the flooring and backing.

2 Remove the flooring strip by strip. Wrap one end around a rolling pin or piece of tubing, then roll up the strip of flooring material.

3 Scrape away any remaining backing or adhesive, using a long-handled floor scraper. When needed, use a trisodium phosphate (TSP) solution to loosen residue. Wear rubber gloves.

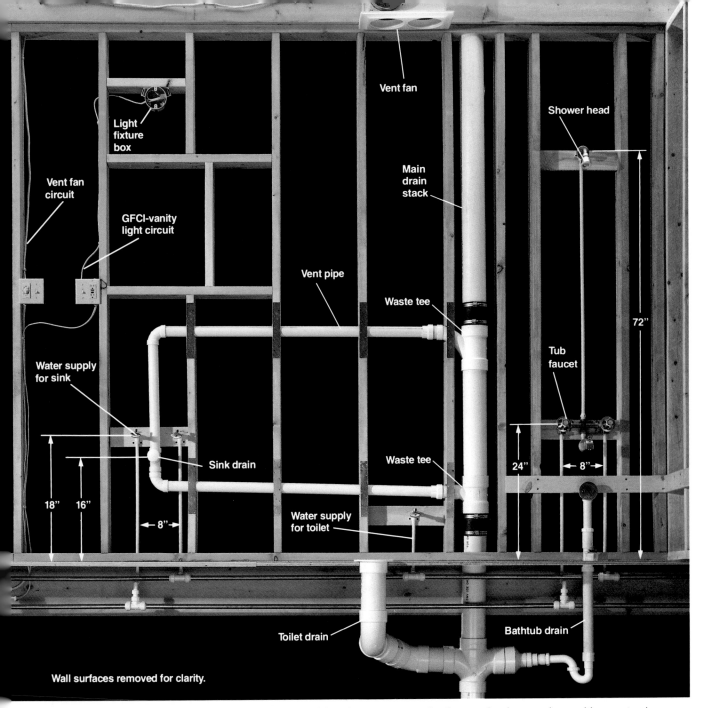

Vent fan

Shower head

Light
fixture
box

Main
drain
stack

Vent fan
circuit

GFCI-vanity
light circuit

Vent pipe

Waste tee

Tub
faucet

72"

Water supply
for sink

Sink drain

Waste tee

24"   ← 8" →

18"   16"

Water supply
for toilet

← 8" →

Toilet drain

Bathtub drain

Wall surfaces removed for clarity.

A basic rough-in for framing, wiring, and plumbing in an average bathroom is shown above. Your actual rough-in will vary, depending on the layout of your bathroom fixtures.

Roughing-in the Bathroom

Install new framing, plumbing, and electrical lines, called the "rough-in," while wall cavities are uncovered.

Doing your own rough-in work requires some experience. Many remodelers with limited wiring and plumbing experience hire professionals to install new pipes and electrical cable, then connect the fixtures themselves.

If your project requires a building permit (pages 14 to 15), make sure the building inspector approves the rough-in work before you finish the walls.

This section shows:

• Working with framing (pages 44 to 45)
• Adding new plumbing pipes (pages 46 to 51)
• Installing electrical cable & boxes (pages 52 to 55)

Framing for a basement bathroom:
Basements in newer houses often contain drain and water supply stub-outs for a sink, shower, and toilet. To finish the basement bathroom, frame around the existing stub-outs, and extend water supply pipes and drain pipes as needed. Floor drain stub-outs may be framed with 2 × 4s and buried under gravel fill (photo below), or may extend through the concrete floor (page 59).

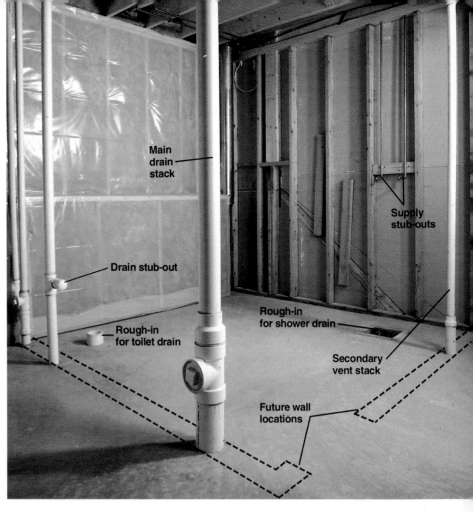

Main drain stack

Supply stub-outs

Drain stub-out

Rough-in for shower drain

Rough-in for toilet drain

Secondary vent stack

Future wall locations

Rough-in Framing Variations

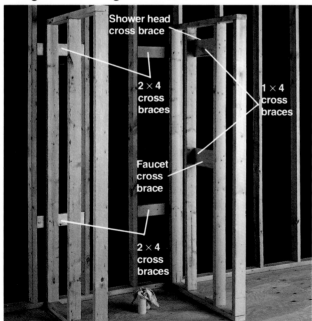

Shower head cross brace

2 × 4 cross braces

1 × 4 cross braces

Faucet cross brace

2 × 4 cross braces

Build a shower alcove using 2 × 4 partition walls. Several 2 × 4 cross braces between existing studs help anchor the shower alcove and any nailing strips that will be added for attaching wall surfaces. The 1 × 4 cross braces within the alcove frame help anchor the faucet and shower head. See pages 64 to 67 for directions on building a shower stall.

Access panel openings

Build a frame for a bathtub or whirlpool using short 2 × 4 stud walls topped with a plywood deck. The hole in the deck should be slightly smaller than the tub rim flanges. The deck frame should include extra studs to frame access panel openings. See pages 76 to 77 for directions on building a deck for a whirlpool tub.

43

Framing a new bathroom wall: Use 2 × 6 lumber to build new plumbing walls (walls that contain drain or supply pipes). The extra thickness allows you to cut notches or drill holes for drain pipe without weakening the weight-bearing capacity of the wall.

Adding pipe in existing framing: Cut notches or drill holes in 2 × 4 wall studs to make room for plumbing pipes, then attach 2 × 2 furring strips to each stud in the wall. The strips provide a nailing surface for wall coverings and add strength to the wall.

Working with Framing

Many bathroom fixtures require special framing work. Common framing projects include shower stall frames, bathtub and whirlpool decks, frames for recessed cabinets, and installing cross braces to support plumbing or bathroom fixtures. Complete all framing work before you install new fixtures and surface materials.

In bathrooms, the structural elements of floors and walls are highly prone to water damage. Inspect framing members and subfloors carefully, especially if wall or floor surfaces show signs of discoloration, cracking, or peeling. Locate the source of any damage, such as a leaky pipe, and correct the problem before you replace or reinforce damaged wood.

If several framing members are warped, bowed, or deteriorated, your house may have a serious structural problem that should be evaluated by a building inspector or a licensed building contractor.

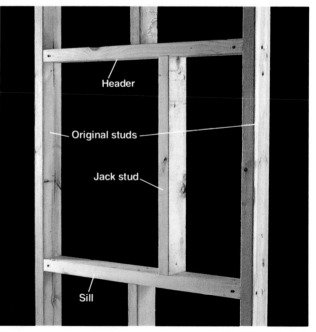

Header

Original studs

Jack stud

Sill

Frame an opening for a recessed cabinet by cutting away wall studs with a reciprocating saw or hand saw, then installing a header, sill, and jack studs as needed. Follow the cabinet manufacturer's specifications for rough-opening size.

Solving Common Bathroom Framing Problems

Replace damaged sections of subfloor: Remove old underlayment, then cut out damaged areas of subfloor, exposing some nailing surface on joists that border the cutout. Measure hole, then cut and install a plywood patch the same thickness as the subfloor. Install new underlayment (page 95) before laying new floor covering.

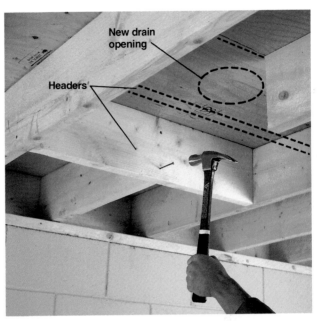

Frame a new toilet drain opening: If your project requires that you relocate the toilet, to frame the new opening you may need to cut away a section of floor joist and nail headers in place. Always support the floor joist from below while you cut and install headers.

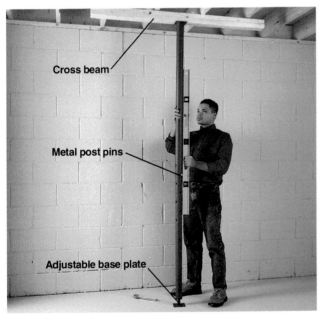

Raise sagging floor joists: Install a support post and cross beam below the sagging bathroom floor. Adjust the post to rough height, using metal pins, then position the post so it is plumb. Raise post by turning the threaded base plate; pressure will hold the post and beam in place. Raise no more than 1/2" per day, until floor above is level. Building Codes may restrict use of adjustable posts, so consult an inspector.

Reinforce framing members: Attach a "sister" alongside the existing joist or stud, using 3" lag screws. The sister should run the full length of the old framing member. Sisters should be installed wherever existing framing members are damaged, and may be required under floor areas that will support bathtubs or whirlpools. A temporary post and cross beam can be useful for holding joists while they are screwed together.

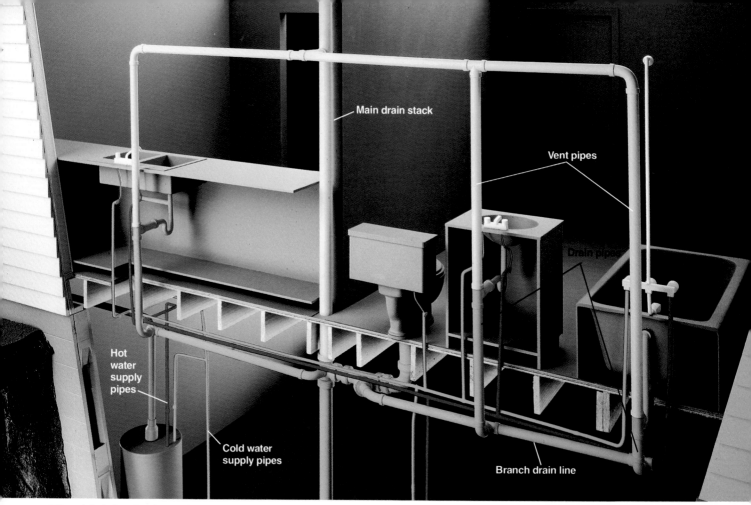

Main drain stack

Vent pipes

Drain pipes

Hot
water
supply
pipes

Cold water
supply pipes

Branch drain line

Plumbing for bathroom fixtures includes supply pipes that carry water to the fixtures, and drain pipes that carry waste water to branch drains and the main drain stack. Branch drain lines that are longer than 3 ft., 6" require a vent pipe that loops back to the main drain stack. Vent pipes equalize pressure in the drain lines, preventing the creation of a partial vacuum that may siphon standing water from drain traps. Without standing water in the drain traps, dangerous sewer gases may enter your house.

Adding New Plumbing Pipes

Most major bathroom remodeling projects require some changes or additions to supply pipes and drain pipes. Use plastic drain and supply pipes when adding new plumbing lines to an existing system, unless your Building Code restricts the use of plastic. Plastic pipe is inexpensive, easy to work with, and can be connected to any type of metal pipe, using common transition fittings (see page 48).

Everything You Need:

Tools: tape measure, reciprocating saw, pipe cutter, level, screwdriver, hammer, utility knife, drill with spade bit.

Materials: plastic pipe and fittings, masking tape, solvent glue, emery cloth, pipe straps, metal protector plates.

Remove a section of wall, if necessary, to gain access to existing plumbing lines. Remove enough wall surface to reveal half of the stud face at each side of the opening, providing a nailing surface so the wall can be patched easily when plumbing work is completed.

Tips for Adding New Plumbing Pipes

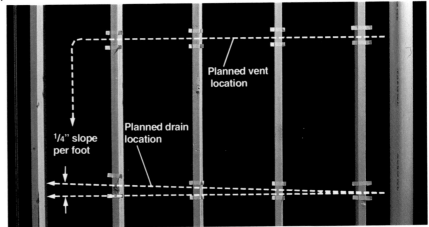

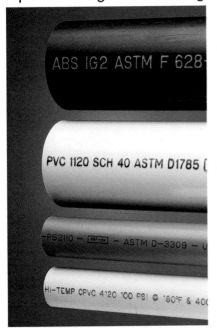

Plastic pipe types are identified by imprinted grade stamps. For drain pipe, use PVC or ABS. For supply pipe, use CPVC or PB.

Plan drain lines in walls so they slope down toward the main drain stack or branch drain at a rate of 1/4" per foot. Fixtures located more than 3 ft., 6" from the branch drain or drain stack must also be connected to a vent pipe that joins the main stack or exits through the roof.

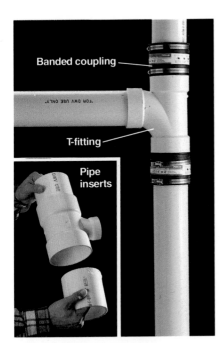

Use banded couplings and T-fittings to connect pipes to the main drain stack. Solvent-glue a pipe insert into each end of a T-fitting (inset), then slip a banded coupling over each cut end of the main stack. Insert the T-fitting into the space between the couplings, draw sleeves of couplings over T-fitting, and secure metal bands.

Protect pipes from punctures, if they are less than 1 1/4" from front face of wall studs, by attaching metal protector plates to the framing members.

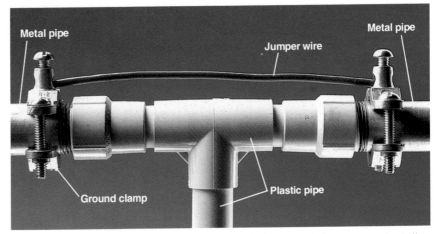

CAUTION: Install a jumper wire and ground clamps whenever you install new plastic pipe that interrupts a section of metal pipe. In many homes, the electrical system is grounded through the metal plumbing system; jumper wires are a safety feature that keep the grounding route intact.

Basic Plumbing Fittings

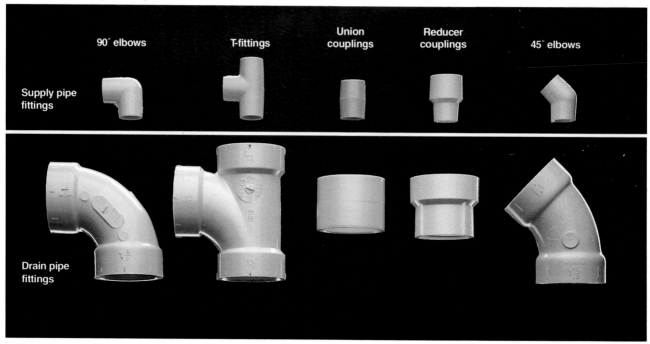

| | 90° elbows | T-fittings | Union couplings | Reducer couplings | 45° elbows |

Supply pipe fittings

Drain pipe fittings

Use plastic fittings and solvent glue to connect lengths of pipe. Common fittings include (from left): 90° elbows, T-fittings, union couplings, reducer couplings, and 45° elbows.

How to Connect Plastic Pipes to Metal Pipes

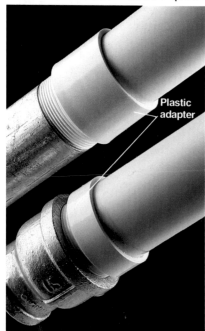

Plastic adapter

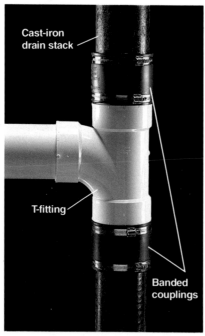

Cast-iron drain stack

T-fitting

Banded couplings

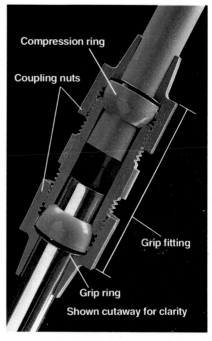

Compression ring

Coupling nuts

Grip fitting

Grip ring

Shown cutaway for clarity

To threaded metal: Screw a plastic adapter onto a threaded metal pipe (top) or into a threaded metal fitting (bottom). Wrap Teflon® tape around pipe threads to improve the seal. After the threaded connection is made, solvent-glue the plastic pipe to the plastic adapter.

To cast iron: Install banded couplings and a T-fitting (page 47). Cast-iron waste stacks are very heavy, and should be supported while being cut.

To copper: Insert copper and plastic pipes into opposite ends of a plastic grip fitting. To create a firm connection, tighten the coupling nut at each end of the grip fitting. Do not overtighten.

How to Connect Plastic Pipe

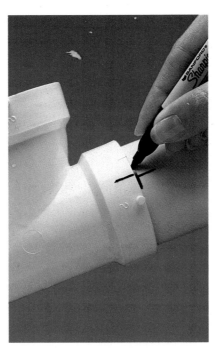

1 Cut plastic pipe to desired length, using a hacksaw, pipe cutter, or a miter saw. Use a utility knife to remove rough burrs on the cut ends.

2 Test-fit the pipes and fittings to make sure the pipes fit tightly against the bottom of the fitting sockets. Make alignment marks across each joint with a pen, then separate the pipes and fittings.

3 Clean the pipe ends and the insides of the fitting sockets with emery cloth.

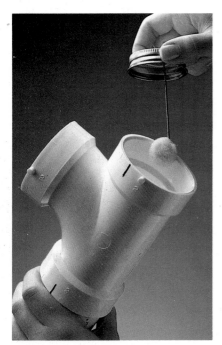

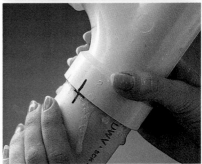

4 Apply plastic pipe primer to the pipe end and to the inside of the fitting socket. Primer dulls glossy surfaces and ensures a good seal.

5 Apply a thick coat of solvent glue to the pipe end, and a thin coat to the inside of the fitting socket. Solvent glue hardens in about 30 seconds, so work fast.

6 Insert the pipe into the fitting so alignment marks (step 2) are offset slightly, then twist the pipe until the marks meet. Hold the joint together for 20 seconds, then wipe off excess glue. Allow 30 minutes for the glue to set.

How to Install Drain Pipe for a Sink

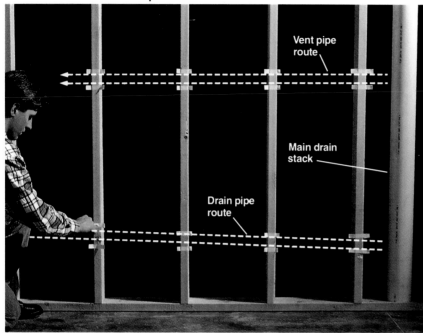

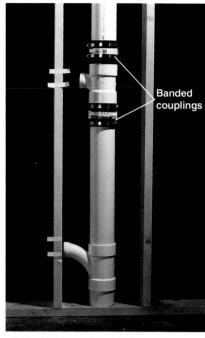

1 Mark the route for the new drain pipe on the wall studs, using masking tape. Drain pipe should slope down toward the main drain stack at a rate of ¼" per foot. If new drain line is over 3 ft., 6" long, a separate vent pipe is required (see pages 46 and 47). Install a 1 × 4 cross brace between studs where drain stub-out will be located.

2 Install transition fittings for connecting new plastic pipes to existing drain pipes. Use banded couplings to make connections to the main drain stack.

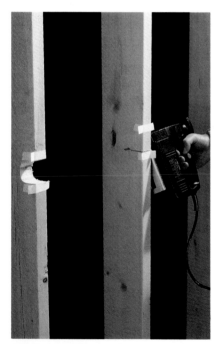

3 Cut notches or holes in the framing members along the marked route for the pipes (see page 44).

4 Cut and test-fit new pipes and fittings. When satisfied with the layout, make alignment marks and solvent-glue the pieces together permanently (page 49). After the joints have set at least 30 minutes, anchor pipe to cross braces, using pipe straps.

5 Attach metal protector plates across the front of framing members to protect the pipes from punctures.

How to Install Water Supply Pipes

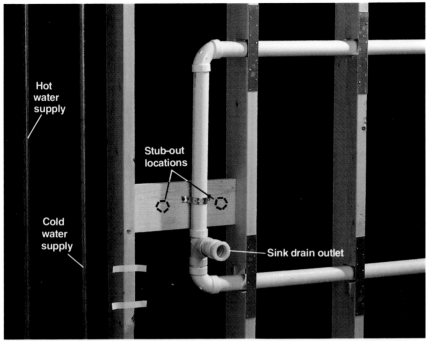

Hot
water
supply

Cold
water
supply

Stub-out
locations

Sink drain outlet

1 Mark the location of new water supply pipes on the wall studs, using masking tape. Water supply stub-outs generally are centered around the drain outlet, spaced about 8" apart. The stub-out for the hot water line should be on the left side of the drain stub-out, and the cold water line should be on the right. Shut off main water supply, and run faucets to drain plumbing lines.

2 Drill holes through the centers of framing members to hold new plastic water supply pipes. New pipes must not be larger in diameter than the existing water supply pipes.

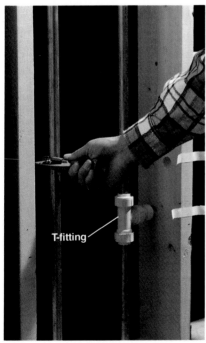

T-fitting

3 Cut out sections of existing supply pipes, using a pipe cutter, and install T-fittings for connecting new plastic pipes.

4 Cut and test-fit plastic supply pipes and fittings. When you are satisfied with the pipe layout, solvent-glue the pieces together.

5 Attach the new pipes to the cross brace, using pipe straps, then attach shutoff valves to the ends of the pipes. (Some shutoff valves are solvent-glued, others use compression fittings.)

Installing Electrical Cable & Boxes

Running electrical cable through walls and installing new electrical boxes is not difficult, but unless you have plenty of wiring experience, hire an electrician to make wiring connections at fixtures and at the main service panel.

Working with wiring is easier if the wall surfaces are removed, but installing new wiring in finished walls is possible if you use retrofit electrical boxes (see photo below) and special tools for retrofit wiring (see pages 54 to 55).

Always be aware of Electrical Code, permit, and inspection issues when working with wiring. The list on the opposite page shows general electrical requirements for bathrooms, but consult a local inspector for requirements in your area.

Everything You Need:

Tools: drill, chisel, hammer, screwdriver, utility knife, cable ripper, wire stripper, fish tape.

Materials: electrical tape, electrical boxes, NM cable, wire nuts, cable staples.

Wiring Variations

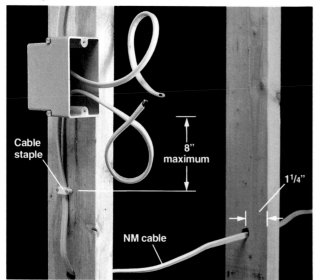

For new framing: Attach plastic electrical boxes to the framing members so the front face of each box will be flush with the wall surface. Anchor NM (non-metallic) sheathed cable to framing members with cable staples driven no more than 4 ft. apart, and within 8" of electrical boxes. Run cable through framing members by drilling 5/8" holes, set back at least 1 1/4" from the front of the framing members.

For finished walls: Install retrofit electrical boxes with internal cable clamps (inset). To run cable across framing members, cut access holes (page 54) in the wall surface at each framing member, and cut a notch in the framing member. Thread the cable between the holes, and position it in notches. Cover the cable with metal protector plates before patching holes.

Requirements for Wiring a Bathroom

The requirements listed below are for general information only. Contact your local electrical inspector for specific wiring regulations.

• Each bathroom should be serviced by at least one 15-amp circuit that does not supply power to any other room. Only light fixtures, receptacles, and vent fans without heating elements should be powered by this circuit.

• Each heating appliance, like a wall heater or an overhead heat lamp, should be powered by a separate, dedicated circuit.

• Whirlpool motors must be powered by a dedicated circuit protected by a GFCI (ground-fault circuit-interrupter). Local Code may require that wiring for a whirlpool tub be done by a licensed electrician.

• At least one light fixture that is controlled by a wall switch must be installed.

• All receptacles must be GFCI-protected.

• Vanity light fixtures cannot contain built-in electrical receptacles.

• Wall switches must be at least 60" away from bathtubs and showers.

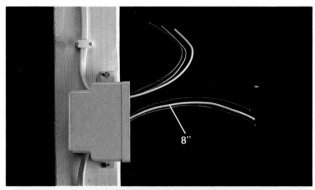

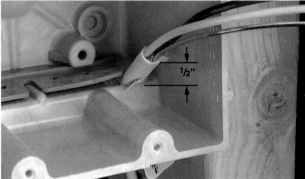

Extend wire at least 8" beyond the front face of electrical boxes (top photo). Cables should have at least 1/2" of outer sheathing extending intact into the box (bottom photo). The sheathing protects the cable wires from possible damage caused by the clamp.

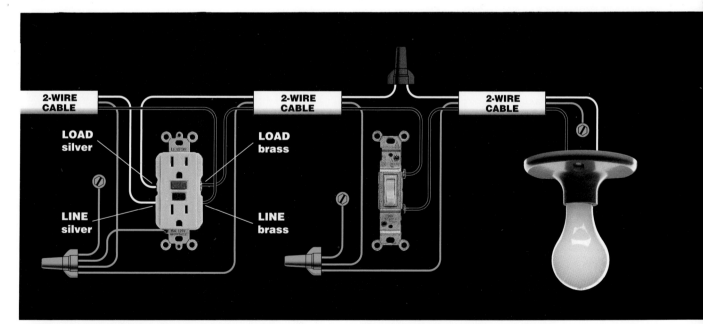

A common bathroom circuit begins with a 2-wire, 14-gauge NM cable (sold as 14-2 NM) that runs from the main service panel to a GFCI receptacle. From the GFCI receptacle, the circuit runs to a wall switch, sometimes mounted in the same electrical box. Another length of 2-wire cable runs from the wall switch to a light fixture, often mounted on a wall above the vanity. In the circuit shown above, all wiring passes through the GFCI receptacle, providing shock protection for the entire circuit. A vent fan with heater (page 114), whirlpool (page 75), electric heater, and any other major appliance each requires its own dedicated electrical circuit.

How to Install Cables & Electrical Boxes in Finished Walls

1 Make cutouts for electrical boxes. To mark a cutout area, position the box, then outline with a pencil. Shut off power. Drill a pilot hole at one corner of the outline, then complete the cutout with a wallboard saw or jig saw.

2 Plan a route for running cable between electrical boxes. Where cable must cross framing members, cut an access opening in the wall or ceiling surface, then cut a notch into the framing member with a wood chisel.

3 Insert a fish tape (a semi-rigid wire used to pull cables) through the access hole (top photo), and extend it until it pokes out of the cutout for the new electrical box (bottom photo).

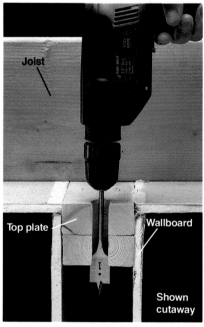

If there is access to ceiling joists above the cutout area, drill a 1" hole down through the top plate and into the wall cavity, using a spade bit. Extend a fish tape through the hole and to the nearest wall cutout.

4 Trim back 3" of sheathing from the end of the cable, then insert the wires through the loop at the end of a fish tape.

5 Bend the wires back against the cable sheathing, then use electrical tape to bind the wires tightly to the fish tape. Pull the fish tape and cable out through the access hole. Detach the cable from the fish tape.

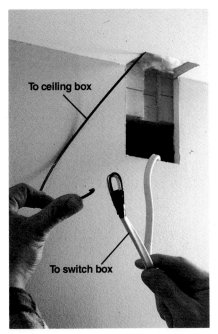

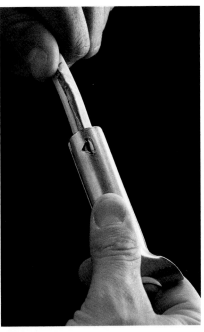

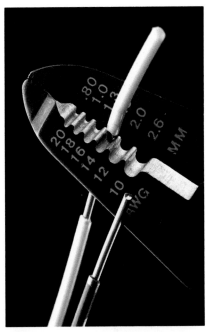

6 Use the fish tape to pull the cable through the remaining access openings until the entire cable run has been completed.

7 Cut cable so at least 18" remains at each end of the cable run, then use a cable ripper to strip back 12" of sheathing from each end.

8 Use a wire stripper to remove 3/4" of insulation from the end of each wire, at both ends of the cable run.

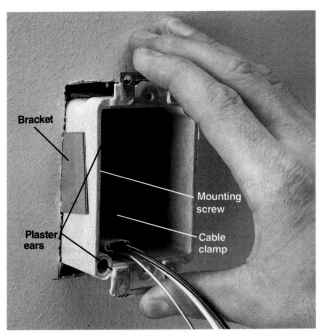

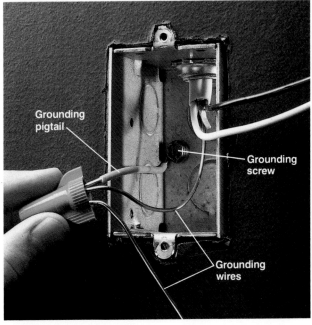

9 Insert cables into the retrofit box, then tighten the cable clamp. Insert the retrofit box into the cutout, flush against the wall surface. Tighten the mounting screw in the rear of the box. This causes the bracket on the back side of the box to draw the "plaster ears" of the mounting flange tight against the wall surface.

Metal boxes only: Connect a green, insulated pigtail wire to the grounding screw at the back of the electrical box. Join the other end of the pigtail and all other grounding wires together, using a green wire nut.

Bathroom Remodeling Projects

Select the shower, bathtub, or whirlpool first when planning your new bathroom. These fixtures, available in a limited range of colors and styles, set the tone for an entire room. Sinks, cabinets, tile, and accessories are available in many styles and colors, and can be matched easily to a new tub or whirlpool.

Installing Showers, Bathtubs & Whirlpools

Installing and hooking up plumbing for bathtubs and showers is a fairly simple job. Whirlpools are more complicated because they also require electrical hookups.

The most difficult task when installing tubs, showers, and whirlpools is moving these bulky fixtures up stairways and through narrow doorways. With a two-wheel dolly and a little help, however, the job is much easier. Measure your doorways and hallways to make sure that any large fixture you buy will fit through them.

If you do not plan to remove and replace your wall surfaces, you still should cut away at least 6" of wall surface above the tub or whirlpool, allowing easier access for installing fixtures.

This section shows:

- Installing showers (pages 62 to 67)
- Installing bathtubs (pages 68 to 72)
- How to install a tub surround (page 73)
- Installing whirlpools (pages 74 to 79)

Tips for Installing Showers, Bathtubs & Whirlpools

Choose the correct tub for your plumbing set-up. Alcove-installed tubs with only one side apron are sold as either "left-hand" or "right-hand" models, depending on the location of the predrilled drain and overflow holes in the tub. To determine which type you need, face into the alcove and look to see if the tub drain will be on your right or your left.

Install extra floor support if the floor joists below the planned bathtub or whirlpool location are too small, or spaced too far apart. Generally, you should attach additional "sister" joists under the tub area (page 45) if your current joists are 2 × 10 or smaller, or if they are more than 16" apart. If you are unsure about structural support issues, contact a building inspector or a professional contractor.

Add fiberglass insulation around the body of a bathtub to reduce noise and conserve heat. Before setting the tub in position, wrap unfaced batting around the tub, and secure it with string or twine. For showers and deck-mounted whirlpools, insulate between framing members.

Chisel out mortar around plumbing stub-outs set into basement floors, to make room for drain fittings that slip over the drain pipe. Use a masonry hammer and masonry chisel, directing the blows away from the pipe, until you have exposed the pipe about 1" below floor level. Wear eye protection.

Shower & Tub Styles

Shower panels are used to make simple, inexpensive shower stalls. The individual shower panels usually are joined together into a three-sided stall unit, then bonded to the walls of a framed shower alcove.

Neo-angle shower stalls occupy less floor space than full-square corner stalls. Neo-angle shower bases are included in some shower surround kits, and they also are sold as bases for custom-built shower stalls.

Custom shower stalls are built to fit unusual spaces or to meet specific color or style needs. Because they usually are made with ceramic tile or tempered glass, installing custom shower stalls can be tricky and fairly expensive.

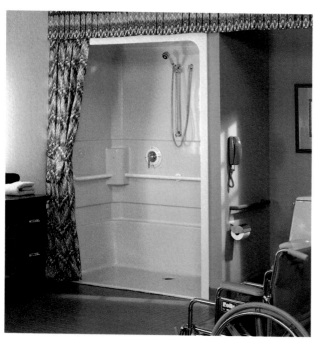

Barrier-free shower stalls are designed for elderly or physically challenged users. Most models have a very low curb, or no curb at all. Barrier-free shower stalls usually are wider than standard shower stalls, and many have a built-in shower seat and two shower heads.

Tub surround panels transform a plain bathtub into a combination tub-shower. They are a good choice for remodeling, because they are easy to get through existing doorways. Paneled tub surrounds are composed of three, five, or seven panels that are installed with panel adhesive.

Alcove whirlpools and tubs are surrounded on three sides by permanent walls, and most have an apron on the front side. Most alcove tubs and whirlpools can be converted to a shower by adding tub surround panels.

Deck-mounted whirlpools and tubs rest on the bathroom subfloor, in a bed of mortar. They are surrounded by a custom-made tub deck or platform. A deck can be attached to one or more bathroom walls, or it can be a freestanding "island." Adding a wide deck gives the tub a "sunken" appearance.

Freestanding whirlpools and tubs are available in both modern and traditional "claw-foot" styles. Although they require little installation work, freestanding tubs are made from heavy cast iron and are difficult to move. Because plumbing is exposed, choose pipes with an attractive finish.

One-piece tub and shower units can be timesavers—if you can get them into your bathroom. Be sure to measure doorways carefully before purchasing a one-piece unit. Due to their seamless construction, one-piece units are virtually leakproof.

Installing Showers

Use prefabricated shower panels and a plastic shower base to build an inexpensive, easy-to-install shower stall. For an elegant look and greater durability, you may prefer a custom-tiled shower stall.

Building Codes require that each home have a tub in at least one bathroom, but in spare bathrooms or guest baths, you can replace the tub with a shower stall to create space for storage or a second sink.

Everything You Need:

Tools: marker, level, channel-type pliers, hacksaw, hole saw, drill, caulk gun.

Materials: 2 × 4, 1 × 4 lumber, 10d nails, pipe straps, shower pipes & fittings, dry-set mortar, soap, wood screws, wallboard screws, panel adhesive, carpet scrap, tub & tile caulk.

Ceramic tile for custom showers is installed the same way as ceramic wall tile (pages 86 to 93). Ceramic shower accessories are mortared in place during the tile installation.

Optional Shower Features

Anti-scald valves protect against sudden water temperature changes. Most types use a water-pressure regulator (left). Once installed, faucets with anti-scald valves look like standard faucets (right).

Storage cabinet with sliding doors holds bathing accessories. Some shower-surround panels have cabinets already built in.

Anatomy of a Shower

Shower stalls are available in many different sizes and styles, but the basic elements are the same. Most shower stalls have a supply system, a drain system, and a framed shower alcove.

The supply system: The shower head and shower arm extend out from the wall, where they are connected to the shower pipe with an elbow fitting. The shower pipe rises up from the faucet body, which is supplied by hot and cold supply pipes, and is controlled by a faucet handle and shutoff valves.

The drain system: The drain cover attaches to the drain tailpiece. A rubber gasket on the tailpiece slips over the drain pipe, leading to the P-trap and the branch drain.

Shower stall: A layer of mortar is applied to the subfloor to create a bed for the shower base. Water-resistant wallboard or cementboard is attached to the stall framing members to provide a surface for gluing shower panels.

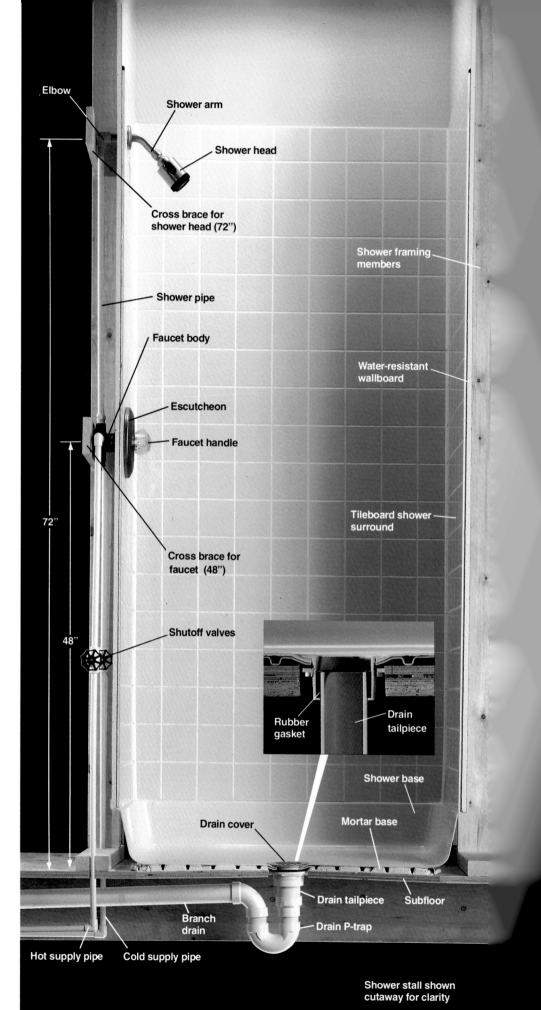

Elbow

Shower arm

Shower head

Cross brace for shower head (72")

Shower framing members

Shower pipe

Faucet body

Water-resistant wallboard

Escutcheon

Faucet handle

72"

Tileboard shower surround

Cross brace for faucet (48")

48"

Shutoff valves

Rubber gasket

Drain tailpiece

Shower base

Drain cover

Mortar base

Drain tailpiece

Subfloor

Branch drain

Drain P-trap

Hot supply pipe

Cold supply pipe

Shower stall shown cutaway for clarity

How to Frame a Shower Alcove

1 Measure shower base, and mark its dimensions on the floor. Measure from center of drain pipe to ensure that drain will be centered in the shower alcove. Install blocking between studs in existing walls to provide a surface for anchoring the alcove walls.

2 Build 2 × 4 alcove walls just outside the marked lines on the floor. Anchor the alcove walls to the existing wall and the sub-floor. If necessary, drill holes or cut notches in the sole plate for plumbing pipes.

3 In the stud cavity that will hold the shower faucet and shower head, mark reference points 48" and 72" above the floor to indicate location of the faucet and shower head.

4 Attach 1 × 4 cross braces between studs to provide surfaces for attaching shower head and faucet. Center the cross braces on the marked reference points, and position them flush with the back edge of the studs to provide adequate space for the faucet body (inset) and shower head fittings.

5 Following manufacturer's directions, assemble plumbing pipes and attach faucet body and shower-head fitting to cross braces. (See pages 46 to 49 for information on working with plastic plumbing pipes.) Attach the faucet handle and shower head after the shower panels have been installed (pages 66 to 67).

How to Install a Shower Base

1 Trim the drain pipe in the floor to the height recommended by the manufacturer (usually near or slightly above floor level). Stuff a rag into the drain pipe, and leave it in until you are ready to make the drain connections.

2 Prepare the shower drain piece as directed by the manufacturer, and attach it to the drain opening in the shower base (see inset photo, page 63). Tighten locknut securely onto drain tailpiece to ensure a waterproof fit.

Locknut Sealing gasket

Drain tailpiece

3 Mix a batch of dry-set mortar, then apply a 1" layer to the subfloor, covering the shower base area. Mortar stabilizes and levels the shower base.

4 Apply soap to the outside of the drain pipe in the floor, and to the inside of the rubber gasket in the drain tailpiece. Set the shower base onto the drain pipe, and press down slowly until the rubber gasket in the drain tailpiece fits snugly over the drain pipe.

5 Press the shower base down into the dry-set mortar, carefully adjusting it so it is level. If directed by manufacturer, anchor the shower base with screws driven through the edge flanges and into the wall studs. Let mortar dry for 6 to 8 hours.

Edge flanges

How to Install a Shower Panel Kit

1 Attach the shower dome, if included with the shower panel kit, to the walls of the shower alcove. Refer to the manufacturer's directions for exact installation height for the dome.

2 Screw the mounting strips for the shower door frame to both sides of the shower opening.

3 Make a template for marking pipe hole locations in shower panels, using the panel kit shipping carton or heavy paper. Mark holes for the shower head and the faucet handle or handles.

4 Lay the template over the shower panel, and drill out holes with a hole saw. Cut larger holes with a jig saw. For more accurate cuts, use plywood to support the panel near the cutout area.

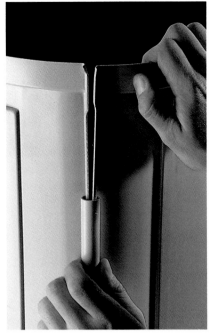  

5 Assemble the shower panels according to manufacturer's directions. Most shower panels are joined together with clips or interlocking flanges before they are installed.

6 Apply heavy beads of panel adhesive to the walls of the shower alcove, and to the mounting strips for the door frame.

7 Slide shower panels into the alcove, and press them against the walls. Pull the panels away from the walls for about 1 minute to let adhesive begin to set, then press the panels back in place.

8 Wedge lengths of scrap lumber between the shower panels to hold the panels in place until the adhesive has set completely. Cover the lumber with scraps of carpeting or rags to avoid damaging the surfaces of the shower panels. Allow the panel adhesive to dry for at least 24 hours before removing the braces.

9 Attach faucet handles, shower arm, and shower head (pages 108 to 111), then caulk the seams between the panels and around the base, using tub & tile caulk (page 124). See page 122 for information on hanging shower doors.

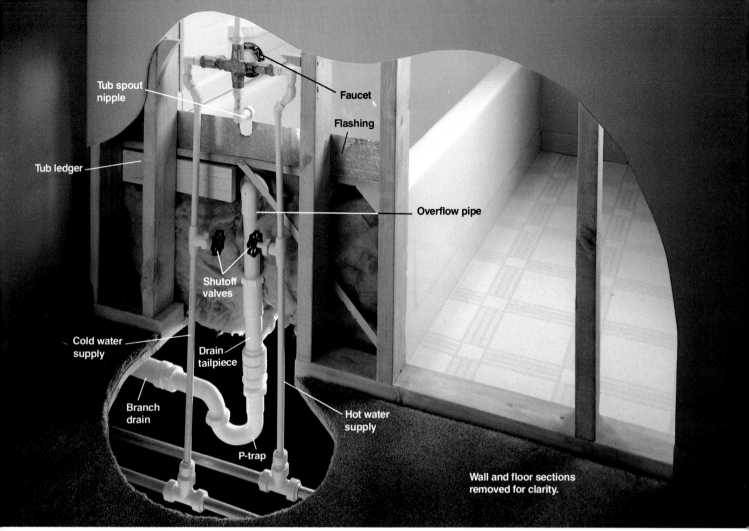

Tub spout nipple

Faucet

Flashing

Tub ledger

Overflow pipe

Shutoff valves

Cold water supply

Drain tailpiece

Branch drain

Hot water supply

P-trap

Wall and floor sections removed for clarity.

The supply system for a bathtub includes hot and cold supply pipes, shutoff valves, a faucet and handles, and a spout. Supply connections can be made before or after the tub is installed.

The drain-waste-overflow system for a bathtub includes the overflow pipe, drain tee, P-trap, and branch drain. The overflow pipe assembly is attached to the tub before installation.

Installing Bathtubs

The development of modern plastic polymers and better construction techniques has created a new generation of tubs that are strong, light, and easy to clean. Even if your old fiberglass or cast-iron tub is in good condition, consider replacing it with a newer model that resists staining and rusting.

Take care when handling a new bathtub, since the greatest chance of damaging the tub occurs during installation. If the inside of your tub has a protective layer of removable plastic, leave it on during installation. Also set a layer of cardboard into the bottom of the tub for added protection while you work.

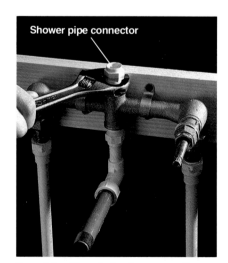

Shower pipe connector

Combination tub-showers: Special faucets have a removable plug in the top. Replace the plug with a shower pipe connector.

Everything You Need:

Tools: channel-type pliers, hacksaw, carpenter's level, pencil, tape measure, saw, screwdriver, drill, adjustable wrench.

Materials: tub protector; shims; galvanized deck screws; drain-waste-overflow kit; 1 × 3, 1 × 4, and 2 × 4 lumber; galvanized roofing nails; galvanized roof flashing; tub & tile caulk.

Tips for Installing Bathtubs

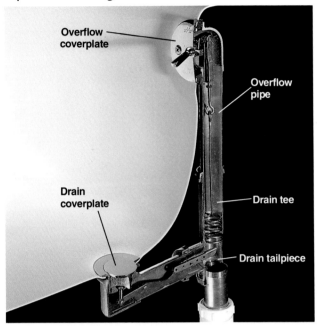

Drain-waste-overflow kit with stopper mechanism must be purchased separately and attached to the tub before it is installed (pages 70 to 71). Available in both brass and plastic types, most kits include an overflow coverplate, an overflow pipe that can be adjusted to different heights, a drain-tee fitting, an adjustable drain tailpiece, and a drain coverplate that screws into the tailpiece.

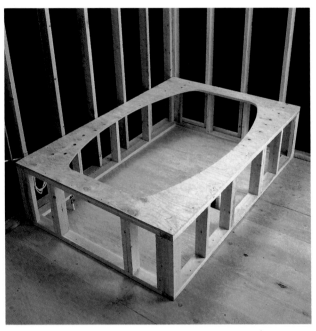

Build a deck for a drop-in style tub or whirlpool (pages 76 to 77). Used frequently with whirlpools, most decks are finished with cementboard and ceramic tile after the tub or whirlpool is installed.

How to Install a Bathtub in an Alcove

1 Attach the faucet body and shower head to the water supply pipes, and attach the assembly to 1 × 4 cross braces (see page 43) before installing the tub. Trim the drain pipe to the height specified by the drain-waste-overflow kit manufacturer.

2 Place a tub-bottom protector, which can be cut from the shipping carton, into the tub. Test-fit the tub by sliding it into the alcove so it rests on the sub-floor, flush against the wall studs.

(continued next page)

3 Check the tub rim with a carpenter's level, and shim below the tub to make it level. Mark the top of the nailing flange at each stud. Remove the bathtub from the alcove.

Measure distance

4 Measure the distance from the top of the nailing flange to the underside of the tub rim (inset), and subtract that amount (usually about 1") from the marks on the wall studs. Draw a line at that point on each wall stud.

5 Cut ledger-board strips, and attach them to the wall studs just below the mark for the underside of the tub rim (step 4). You may have to install the boards in sections to make room for any structural braces at the ends of the tub.

6 Adjust the drain-waste-overflow assembly (usually sold as a separate kit) to fit the drain and overflow openings. Attach gaskets and washers as directed by the manufacturer, then position the assembly against the tub drain and overflow openings.

7 Apply a ring of plumber's putty to the bottom of the drain piece flange, then insert the drain piece through the drain hole in the bathtub. Screw the drain piece into the drain tailpiece, and tighten until snug (page 33). Insert pop-up drain plug.

8 Insert drain plug linkage into the overflow opening, and attach the overflow coverplate with long screws driven into the mounting flange on the overflow pipe. Adjust drain plug linkage as directed by manufacturer.

9 Apply a ½"-thick layer of dry-set mortar to the subfloor, covering the entire area where the tub will rest.

10 Lay soaped 1 × 4 runners across the alcove so they rest on the far sill plate. The runners will allow you to slide the tub into the alcove without disturbing the mortar base.

(continued next page)

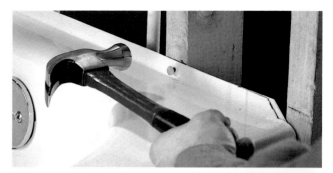

11 Slide the tub over the runners and into position, then remove the runners, allowing the tub to settle into the mortar. Press down evenly on the tub rims until they touch the ledger boards.

12 Before mortar sets, nail the tub rim flanges to the wall studs. Rim flanges are attached either by predrilling holes into the flanges and nailing with galvanized roofing nails (top), or by driving roofing nails into studs so the head of the nail covers the rim flange (bottom). After rim flanges are secured, allow the mortar to dry for 6 to 8 hours.

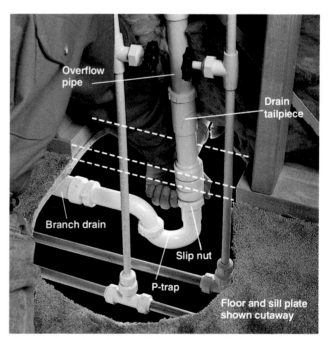

Overflow pipe

Drain tailpiece

Branch drain

Slip nut

P-trap

Floor and sill plate shown cutaway

1/4"

13 Attach 4"-wide strips of galvanized metal roof flashing over the tub flange to help keep water out of the wall. Leave a ¼" expansion gap between the flashing and the tub rim. Nail the flashing to each wall stud, using 1" galvanized roofing nails.

14 Adjust the drain tailpiece so it will fit into the P-trap (you may have to trim it with a hacksaw), then connect it, using a slip nut. Install wall surfaces (pages 82 to 83), then install faucet handles and tub spout (pages 108 to 111). Finally, caulk all around the bathtub (page 124).

How to Install a Tub Surround

1 Mark a cardboard template for the plumbing cutouts, then tape it to the tub surround panel that will cover the plumbing wall. Make the cutouts in the panel with a hole saw or a jig saw.

2 Test-fit surround panels according to manufacturer's suggested installation sequence, and tape them in place. Draw lines along the tops of all the panels, at the outside edges of side panels, and on the tub rim, along the bottoms of panels.

3 Remove panels in reverse order, one at a time. As they are exposed, outline the inside edges of each panel on the surface of the wall.

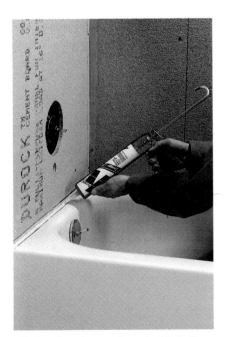

4 Apply a heavy bead of tub & tile caulk to the tub rim, following the marks made where the panels will rest.

5 Apply panel adhesive recommended by manufacturer to the wall in the outline area for the first panel. Carefully press the panel in place.

6 Install the rest of the panels in the proper sequence, following the manufacturer's directions for connecting panels and sealing the seams. Press all the panels in place, then brace for drying (page 67, step 8).

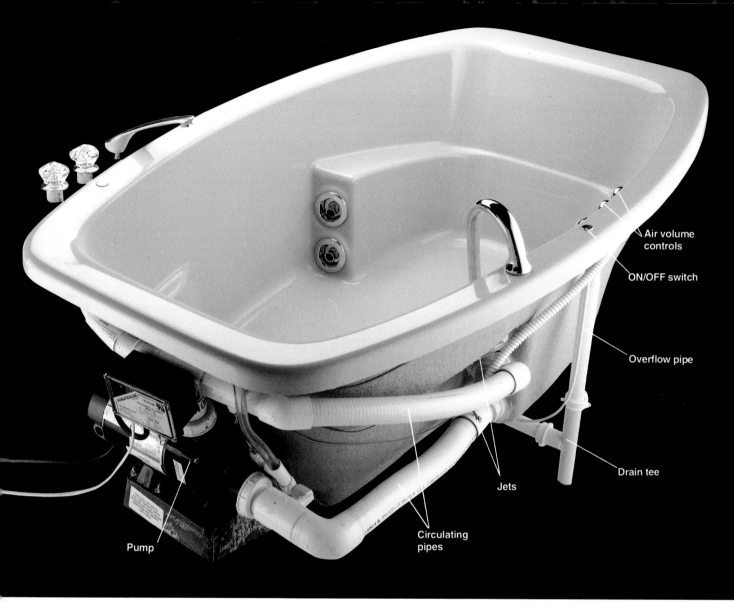

A whirlpool circulates aerated water through jets mounted in the body of tub. Whirlpool pumps move as much as 50 gallons of water per minute to create a relaxing "hydromassage" effect. The pump, pipes, jets, and most of the controls are installed at the factory, making the actual hookup in your home quite simple.

Installing Whirlpools

Installing a whirlpool is very similar to installing a bathtub, once the rough-in is completed. Completing a rough-in for a whirlpool requires that you install a separate electrical circuit for the pump motor. Some Building Codes specify that a licensed electrician be hired to wire whirlpools; check with your local building inspector.

Select your whirlpool before you do rough-in work, because exact requirements will differ from model to model. Select your faucet to match the trim kit that comes with your whirlpool. When selecting a faucet, make sure the spout is large enough to reach over the tub rim. Most whirlpools use "widespread" faucets because the handles and spout are separate, and can be

positioned however you like, even on opposite sides of the tub. Most building centers carry flex tube in a variety of lengths for connecting faucet handles and spout.

Everything You Need:

Tools: marker, tape measure, circular saw, jig saw, drill & spade bits, hacksaw, screwdriver.

Materials: 2 × 4s, 10d nails, ¾" exterior grade plywood, deck screws, dry-set mortar, wood spacer blocks, 8-gauge insulated wire, grounding clamp.

Optional Whirlpool Accessories

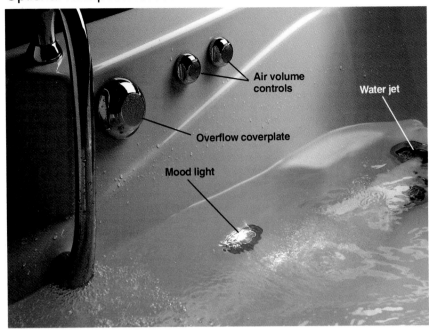

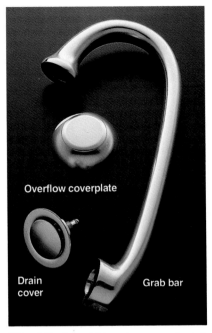

Mood lights are sold as factory-installed accessories by many manufacturers. Most are available with several filters to let you adjust the color to suit your mood. Mood lights are low-voltage fixtures wired through 12-volt transformers. Do not wire mood lights or other accessories into the electrical circuit that supplies the pump motor.

Trim kits for whirlpools are ordered at the time of purchase. Available in a variety of finishes, all of the trim pieces except the grab bar and overflow coverplate normally are installed at the factory.

Requirements for Making Electrical Hookups

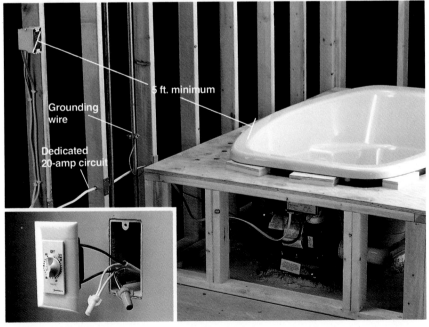

The electrical service for a whirlpool should be a dedicated 115 to 120-volt, 20-amp circuit. The pump motor should be grounded separately, normally to a metal cold water supply pipe. Most whirlpool motors are wired with 12-2 NM cable, but some Local Codes require the use of conduit. **Remote timer switches** (inset), located at least 5 ft. from the tub, are required by some Codes, even for a tub with a built-in timer.

A GFCI circuit breaker at the main service panel is required with whirlpool installations. Always hire an electrician to connect new circuits at your service panel, even if you install the circuit cable yourself.

How to Install a Whirlpool

1 Outline the planned location of the deck frame on the subfloor. Use the plumbing stub-outs as starting points for measuring. Before you begin to build the deck, check the actual dimensions of your whirlpool tub to make sure they correspond to the dimensions listed in the manufacturer's directions. TIP: Plan your deck so it will be at least 4" wide at all points around the whirlpool.

2 Cut top plates, sill plates, and studs for the deck frame. The height of frame should allow 3/4" for the plywood decking, 1/4" for an expansion gap between the deck and the tub rim, and 1" for cementboard, tile, and mortar.

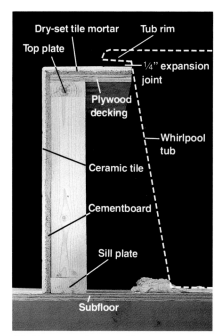

3 Assemble the deck frame. Make sure to leave a framed opening for access panels at the pump location and the drain location. Nail the frame to the floor joists and wall studs or blocking, using 10d nails.

4 Cover the deck frame with 3/4" exterior-grade plywood, and attach with screws spaced every 12". Using a template of the whirlpool cutout (usually included with the tub), mark the deck for cutting. If no template is included, make one from the shipping carton. Cutout will be slightly smaller than the outside dimensions of the whirlpool rim.

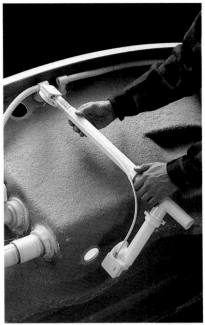

5 Make the cutout hole in the deck, using a jig saw. Drill a pilot hole along the cutout line to start the cut.

6 Measure and mark holes for faucet tailpieces and spout tailpiece according to the faucet manufacturer's suggestions. Drill holes with a spade bit or hole saw.

7 Attach drain-waste-overflow assembly (included with most whirlpools) at the drain and overflow outlets in the tub (pages 70 to 71). Trim the drain pipe in the floor to the proper height.

8 Apply a layer of dry-set mortar to subfloor where tub will rest. Make 12" spacer blocks, 1 1/4" thick (equal to expansion gap, tile, mortar, and cementboard; see step 2). Arrange blocks along the edges of the cutout.

9 With a helper, lift the tub by the rim and set it slowly into the cutout hole. Lower the tub, pressing it into the mortar base, until the rim rests on the spacers at the edges of the cutout area. Avoid moving or shifting the tub once it is in place, and allow the mortar to set for 6 to 8 hours before proceeding with the tub installation. Align the tailpiece of the drain-waste-overflow assembly with the P-trap as you set the tub in place.

(continued next page)

10 Adjust the length of the tailpiece for the drain-waste-overflow assembly, if necessary, then attach assembly to the P-trap in the drain opening, using a slip nut.

11 Inspect the seals on the built-in piping and hoses for loose connections. If you find a problem, contact your dealer for advice. Attempting to fix the problem yourself could void the whirlpool warranty.

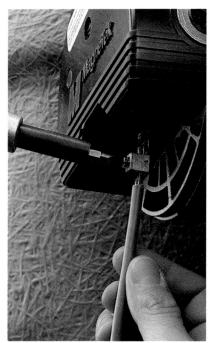

12 With power off, remove the wiring cover from the pump motor. Feed circuit wires from the power source or wall timer into the motor. Connect wires according to directions printed on the motor.

13 Attach an insulated 8-gauge wire to the grounding lug on the pump motor.

14 Attach the other end of the wire to a metal cold water supply pipe in the wall, using a grounding clamp. Test the GFCI circuit breaker.

15 Clean out the tub, then fill it so the water level is at least 3" above the highest water jet.

16 Turn on the pump, and allow it to operate for at least 20 minutes while you check for leaks. Contact your whirlpool dealer if leaks are detected.

17 Staple fiberglass insulation with attached facing to vertical frame supports. Facing should point inward, to keep fibers out of motor. Do not insulate within 6" of pumps, heaters, or lights.

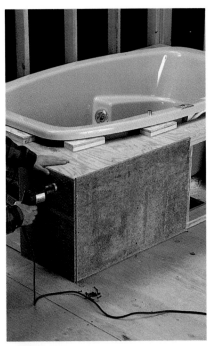

18 Attach cementboard to the sides and top of the deck frame (pages 82 to 83) if you plan to install ceramic tile on the deck. Use ¾" plywood for access panel coverings.

19 Attach finish surfaces to deck and deck frame (pages 86 to 93), then install grab bar (page 121) and the faucet and spout (pages 109 to 111). Fill the joints between floor and deck, and between the tub rim and deck surface, with tub & tile caulk (page 124).

Installing Wall & Floor Surfaces

Common wall surfaces: Water-resistant wallboard (A) can be used in damp areas. It can be painted, covered with vinyl wallcovering, or used as a backing for tub surrounds. Tileboard (B) made of solid PVC resembles ceramic tile, but is installed in panels. PVC tileboard can be installed in any bathroom area. Ceramic tile (C) is water-resistant and durable, and is sold in a wide range of colors, sizes, and styles.

Common floor surfaces: Ceramic floor tile (A) is sold in sizes ranging from 1" × 1" to 12" × 12". A long-lasting product, it is unglazed and thicker than ceramic wall tile. Resilient vinyl tile (B) usually is sold in 12" × 12" squares. Because it has many seams, vinyl tile flooring should be used only in half-baths and other dry areas. Sheet vinyl (C) creates a seamless floor surface that is virtually waterproof.

Create a dramatic change in your bathroom by replacing old wall and floor surfaces. Because of high moisture levels in bathroom areas, it is likely that old wall and floor surfaces are damaged. It is best to replace all wall and floor surfaces, as well as the underlayment and any damaged structural members (pages 38 to 41).

Choose materials and finishes that will stand up to high moisture levels. If available, select products that are designed specifically for bathroom use.

Install new wall surfaces first so you will not damage new floors while finishing the walls. Follow the manufacturer's recommendations for adhesive products and installation techniques. Most floor and wall adhesives are applied with a notched trowel, but some require a caulk gun.

This section shows:

- Installing cementboard & wallboard (pages 82 to 83)
- Installing tileboard (pages 84 to 85)
- Installing ceramic tile (pages 86 to 93)
- Installing flooring (pages 94 to 97)

Tips for Finishing Walls & Floors

Fill dips and knotholes in floors with latex underlayment before installing vinyl flooring. Locate low spots with a long straightedge, then apply underlayment with a large wallboard knife. Let underlayment dry, sand it smooth, then clean the surface thoroughly.

Apply silicone caulk to flanges on bathtubs and shower bases before installing cementboard or water-resistant wallboard. The caulk creates a solid bond and keeps water from seeping into the wall.

Staple a vapor barrier over insulation in exterior bathroom walls or walls that adjoin unheated spaces. The plastic vapor barrier prevents moisture from condensing in the walls.

Patch holes in walls, like those made when installing pipes or wires, using pieces of wallboard cut to fit the openings. Attach small patches to the framing members with hot glue or construction adhesive; attach large patches with wallboard screws. Cover seams with fiberglass wallboard tape and wallboard compound (page 83).

Make access openings in wall surfaces so bathtub and shower fittings and shutoff valves can be reached easily. A whirlpool may require two access panels—one for the drain plumbing and one for the pump motor. Trim the opening with mitered wood moldings, and cover it with a removable plywood panel finished to match the surrounding wall or whirlpool deck.

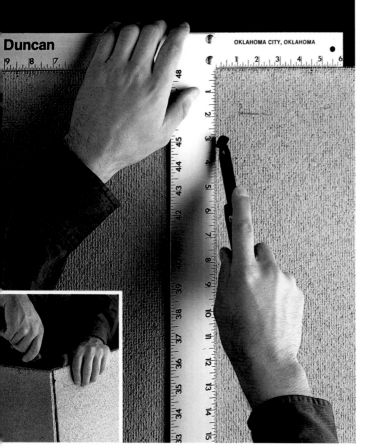

Cut cementboard by scoring the fiberglass surface along cutting line, using a cementboard scoring tool or a utility knife. Snap the panel along the scored line, then cut the back surface (inset).

Installing Cementboard & Wallboard

Installing the appropriate wall surface helps ensure that your new walls last as long as possible. Install new wall surfaces only after you have checked the wall for any structural damage and made repairs, and an inspector has approved all new plumbing and wiring. If bathroom walls are not plumb and square, shim out the studs to ensure that the new wall surface will be flat and straight.

Cementboard and wallboard panels must be supported by studs along the edges. Cut the panels to fit available spaces, or install extra studs to provide surfaces for attaching panels.

Everything You Need:

Tools: utility knife, cementboard scoring tool, chalk, drill, jig saw, screwdriver, hammer, wallboard knife.

Materials: cardboard, fiberglass wallboard tape, wallboard screws and nails, wallboard corner bead, wallboard compound.

Wall Materials for Bathrooms

Choose wall materials appropriate for the moisture levels they must withstand. Standard wallboard (A) is made from a gypsum mineral layer covered with paper on both sides. It can be used in all areas that are not directly exposed to moisture. Water-resistant wallboard (B) is also made from gypsum, but has a water-resistant facing. Use it in wet areas, like behind sinks, and as a backer for tub surrounds or shower panels. Cementboard (C) is a rigid material with a cement core that is faced on both sides with fiberglass. Water does not damage cementboard, making it the best backing material for ceramic tile.

How to Install Wallboard or Cementboard Panels

1 Mark panels for cutouts by coating ends of pipes and edges of electric boxes with chalk or lipstick (top). Position panel, then press it against the pipes to transfer marks (bottom). Make cutouts with a hole saw or jig saw.

2 Make a template from cardboard or heavy paper cut to fit irregular spaces. Use the template to mark cementboard or wallboard panels for cutting, then make cutouts with a jig saw.

3 Attach panels to wall studs with wallboard screws (drill pilot holes in cementboard). Screws should be driven along all panel edges and in the interior wall studs.

4 Cover all seams with fiberglass joint tape. NOTE: If the cementboard or water-resistant wallboard will be used as a backer for tub or shower surround panels, no taping is required.

Finishing wallboard surfaces: Attach metal corner bead to outside corners of wallboard walls, using wallboard nails driven at 8" intervals (left). Apply a thin layer of wallboard compound to all wallboard joints (right) and to nail and screw heads. Let compound dry, sand joints and patches smooth, then wipe clean. The finished wallboard surface may be painted or covered with water-resistant wallcovering.

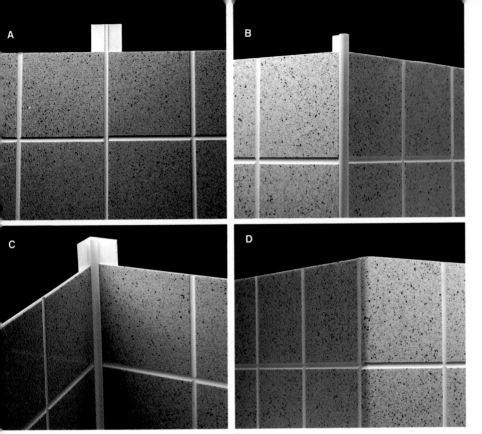

Installing Tileboard

Tileboard looks like ceramic tile, but it is easier to install and is usually less costly. For bathrooms, select tileboard made of solid PVC, rather than laminated hardboard, which can flake and disintegrate when exposed to water.

Tileboard can be installed on any flat, vertical wall surface, including shower or tub areas, but it is not designed to be used on countertops or floors.

Tileboard products are installed as wallcoverings or tub-shower surrounds. The PVC tileboard shown above is installed in 4 × 4 or 5 × 5 panels using a variety of plastic connector strips, including strips for straight vertical seams (A), outside corners (B), and inside corners (C). "Bullnose" tileboard (D) creates smooth corners without connectors.

Everything You Need:

Tools: pencil, tape measure, level, jig saw, drill, hole saw, caulk gun, notched trowel, utility knife.

Materials: cardboard, panel adhesive, tape, caulk, 2 × 4s.

How to Install PVC Tileboard

1 Draw a level reference line on wall to show where the tops of tileboard panels will fit. If floor is uneven, measure up from highest point on the floor so bottoms of panels will fit without trimming.

2 Make cardboard templates for panels that require cutouts or must fit into irregular spaces. Allow space for connector strips in corners and between panels. Align top of template with reference line when marking cutouts.

3 Lay the template over the tileboard panel, and mark holes and cutting lines. See pages 86 to 89 for helpful layout information.

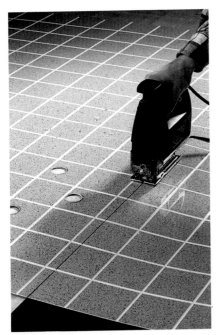

4 Cut tileboard panels along cutting lines with a jig saw. Make cutouts for pipes with a drill and hole saw.

5 Test-fit the panels and connector strips, using tape to attach them to the walls. Outline the position of each panel on the wall, then remove the panels.

6 Apply adhesive recommended by tileboard manufacturer to the wall inside the outline for the first panel. Do not cover the reference lines.

7 Cut connector strips to size for first panel, then spread adhesive on back of strips and attach them to walls. Apply a bead of tub & tile caulk along the inside edges of the connector strips where tileboard panel will fit.

8 Install first tileboard panel by slipping the edges of the panel into the connector strips (inset) as directed by the tileboard manufacturer. Press the entire panel surface to ensure a tight bond, then wipe away any excess caulk and adhesive. Install remaining connector strips and tileboard panels. Gaps near floor will be covered by flooring and baseboard trim (pages 94 to 97).

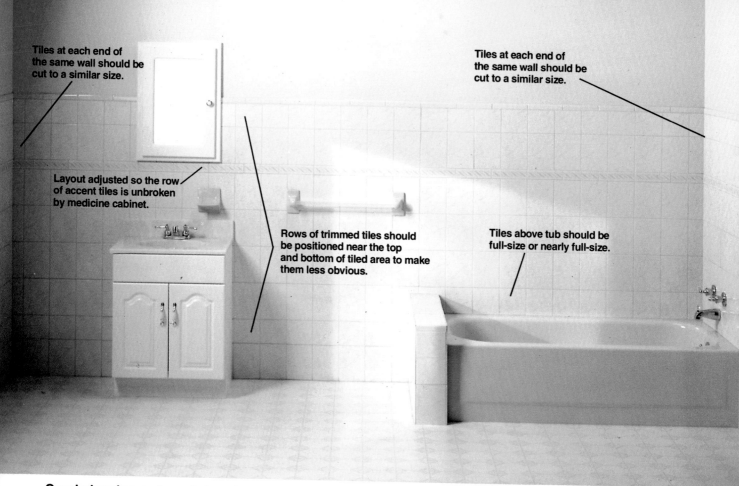

Tiles at each end of the same wall should be cut to a similar size.

Tiles at each end of the same wall should be cut to a similar size.

Layout adjusted so the row of accent tiles is unbroken by medicine cabinet.

Rows of trimmed tiles should be positioned near the top and bottom of tiled area to make them less obvious.

Tiles above tub should be full-size or nearly full-size.

Good planning and careful work are the keys to achieving professional-looking results with ceramic wall tile. The tile project shown above was planned so the tiles directly above the most visible surface (in this bathroom, the bathtub) are nearly full height. To accomplish this, cut tiles were used in the second row up from the floor. The short second row also allows the row of accent tiles to run uninterrupted under the medicine cabinet. Cut tiles in both corners should be of similar width to preserve the symmetrical look of the room.

Installing Ceramic Tile

Ceramic tile is a traditional, custom-installed material frequently used for bathroom walls, shower stalls, and floors (page 94). When properly installed, ceramic tile outlasts most other wall and floor coverings.

Tile is sold in a wide variety of colors, shapes, sizes, and finishes. For most projects, tiles that are at least 4 × 6 are easiest to install because they require less cutting and cover more surface area. Smaller tiles can form more intricate patterns and create safe, nonslip floor surfaces.

To ensure long-lasting results, remove the old wall surface down to the studs, and install a new base layer of cementboard (page 83).

Use a thin layer of dry-set mortar to create a bonding surface for ceramic wall tile. Avoid using the thick beds of standard mortar that were used to set wall tile for many years. Also avoid adhesives or mastics that have no mortar content, because these products do not work well on vertical surfaces.

Everything You Need:

Tools: marker, tape measure, carpenter's level, notched trowel, tile cutter, rod saw, drill with masonry bit, clamps, grout float, sponge, small paint brush, caulk gun.

Materials: straight 1 × 2, dry-set tile mortar with latex additive, ceramic wall tile, ceramic trim tile (as needed), tile grout with latex additive, tub & tile caulk, alkaline grout sealer.

Tips for Planning Tile Layouts

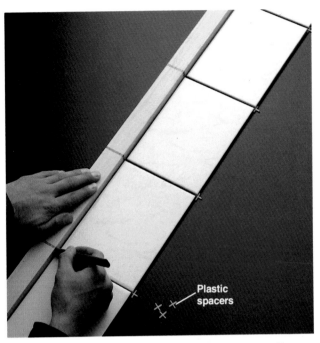

Plastic spacers

Use planning brochures and design catalogs to help you create decorative patterns and borders for your ceramic tile project. Brochures and catalogs are available free of charge from many tile manufacturers.

Make a tile stick to mark layout patterns on walls. To make a tile stick, set a row of tiles (and plastic spacers, if they will be used) in the selected pattern on a flat surface. Mark a straight 1 × 2 to match the tile spacing. Include any narrow trim tiles or accent tiles. If your tiles are square, you will need only one tile stick. For rectangular and odd-shaped tiles, make separate sticks for the horizontal and vertical layouts.

Materials for Tiling Projects

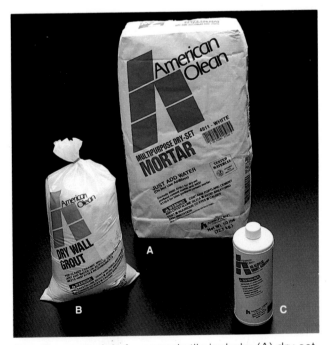

Ceramic tile types include: (A) mosaic tile sheets, (B) 4 × 4 glazed wall tiles with self-spacing edge lugs, (C) textured quarry tiles (natural stone) for floors, and (D) trim tiles for borders and accents.

Bonding materials for ceramic tile include: (A) dry-set mortar, (B) grout mix, and (C) latex grout additive. Latex additive makes grout lines stronger and more crack-resistant.

How to Mark a Layout for Wall Tile

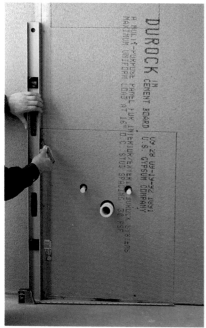

1 Mark the wall to show the planned location of all vanities, wall cabinets, recessed fixtures, and ceramic wall accessories, like soap and toothbrush holders or towel rods.

2 Locate the most visible horizontal line in the bathroom (usually the top edge of the bathtub). Measure up and mark a point at a distance equal to the height of one ceramic tile (if the tub edge is not level, measure up from the lowest spot). Draw a level line through this point, around the entire room. This line represents a tile grout line and is used as a reference line for making the entire tile layout.

3 Use the tile stick to see how the tile pattern will run in relation to other features in the room, like countertops, window and door frames, and wall cabinets. Hold the tile stick so it is perpendicular to the horizontal reference line, with one joint mark touching the line, and note the location of tile joints.

4 Adjust the horizontal reference line if the tile stick shows that tile joints will fall in undesirable spots. In the bathroom shown above, adjusting the reference line downward allows an unbroken row of accent tiles to span the wall under the medicine cabinet (see photo, page 86).

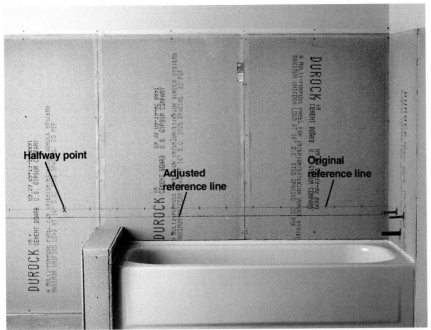

5 On each wall, measure and mark the halfway point along the horizontal reference line (step 4). Using the tile stick as a guide, mark lines in each direction from the halfway point to show where the vertical grout joints will be located. If tile stick shows that corner tiles will be less than 1/2 of full tile width, adjust the layout as shown in next step.

6 Adjust the layout of vertical joints by moving the halfway point (step 5) 1/2 the width of a tile in either direction. Use a carpenter's level to draw a vertical reference line through this point, from the floor to the top tile row.

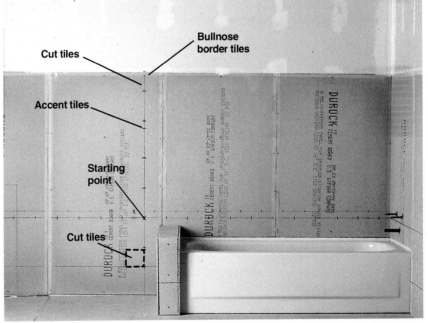

7 Use the tile stick to measure up from the floor along the vertical reference line, a distance equal to the height of one tile plus 1/8", and mark a point on the wall. Draw a level reference line through this point, across the wall.

8 Mark reference lines to show where the remaining tile joints will be located, starting at the point where vertical and horizontal reference lines meet. Include any decorative border or accent tiles. If a row of cut tiles is unavoidable, position it near the floor, between the first and third rows, or at the top, near border tiles. Extend all horizontal reference lines onto adjoining walls that will be tiled, then repeat steps 5 to 8 for all other walls being tiled.

How to Install Ceramic Wall Tile

1 Mark layout pattern (pages 88 to 89), then begin installation with the second row of tiles from the floor. If layout requires cut tiles for this row, mark and cut tiles for the entire row at one time.

2 Make straight cuts with a tile cutter. Place the tile face up on the tile cutter, with one side flush against the cutting guide. Adjust the cutting tool to desired width, then score a groove by pulling the cutting wheel firmly across the tile. Snap the tile along the scored line, as directed by the tool manufacturer.

3 Mix a small batch of dry-set mortar containing a latex additive. (Some mortar has additive mixed in by the manufacturer, and some mortar must have additive mixed in separately.) Cover the back of the first tile with adhesive, using a ¼" notched trowel.

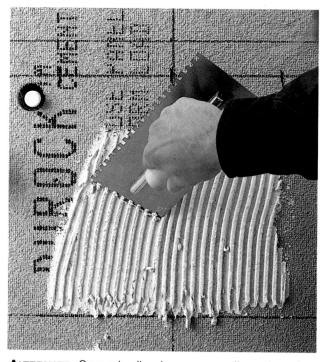

ALTERNATE: Spread adhesive on a small section of the wall, then set the tiles into the adhesive. Dry-set adhesive sets quickly, so work fast if you choose this installation method.

4 Beginning near the center of the wall, apply the tile to the wall with a slight twisting motion, aligning it exactly with the horizontal and vertical reference lines.

5 Continue installing tiles, working from the center to the sides in a pyramid pattern. Make sure to keep tiles aligned with the reference lines. If tiles are not self-spacing, use plastic spacers inserted in the corner joints to maintain even grout lines (inset). The base row should be the last row of full tiles installed.

6 Make notches and curved cuts in tile by clamping the tile to a flat surface, then cutting it with a rod saw (a specialty saw with an abrasive blade designed for cutting tile).

7 As small sections of tile are completed, "set" the tile by laying a scrap 2 × 4 wrapped with carpet onto the tile and rapping it lightly with a mallet. This embeds the tile solidly in the adhesive and creates a flat, even surface.

(continued next page)

8 To mark tiles for straight cuts, begin by taping 1/8" spacers against the surfaces below and to the side of the tile. Position a tile directly over the last full tile installed, then place a third tile so the edge butts against the spacers. Trace the edge of the top tile onto the middle tile to mark it for cutting.

9 Cut holes for plumbing stub-outs by marking the outline of the hole on the tile, then drilling around the edges of the outline, using a ceramic tile bit. Gently knock out the waste material with a hammer. Rough edges of hole will be covered by protective plates on fixtures (called escutcheons).

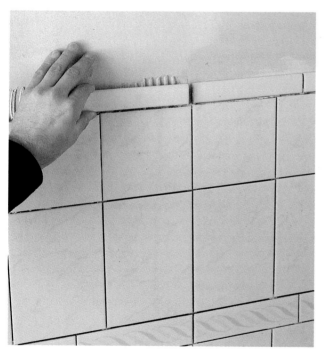

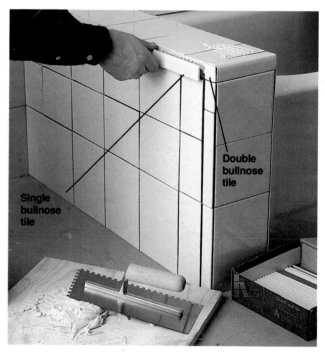

10 Install trim tiles, such as the bullnose edge tiles shown above, at border areas. Wipe away excess mortar along top edge of edge tiles.

11 Use single bullnose and double bullnose tiles at outside corners to cover the rough edges of the adjoining tiles.

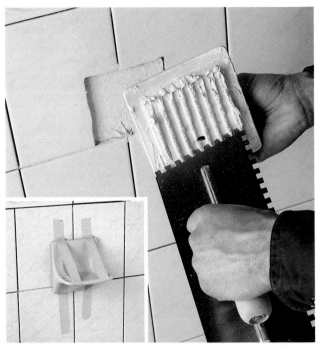

12 Install ceramic accessories by applying dry-set mortar to the back side, then pressing the accessory into place. Use masking tape to hold the accessory in place until the adhesive dries (inset).

13 Let mortar dry completely (12 to 24 hours), then mix a batch of grout containing latex additive. Apply grout with a rubber grout float, using a sweeping motion to force it deep into the joints. Do not grout the joints along the bathtub, floor, and room corners. These expansion joints will be caulked instead.

14 Wipe away excess grout with a damp sponge, then dress the grout lines by drawing a small dowel along all joints.

15 When grout is completely hardened, brush alkaline sealer onto the joints with a small paint brush. Alkaline sealers are better than silicone products for preventing stains and mildew.

16 Seal expansion joints around the bathtub, floor, and room corners with tub & tile caulk (see pages 120, 124). After caulk dries, buff tile with a dry, soft cloth.

Installing Flooring

Sheet vinyl and ceramic tile are the best bathroom flooring materials. Sheet vinyl, when bonded with a full layer of adhesive to sanded plywood underlayment, is an inexpensive and very moisture-resistant material. Do not use highly porous underlayments, like lauan plywood, in bathrooms. Ceramic tile, when set into a bed of dry-set mortar over cementboard underlayment, is attractive and highly durable.

Resilient vinyl floor tiles should be avoided in bathroom remodeling projects, because water easily can seep into the seams between tiles. Carpeting and hardwood are acceptable for dry areas, but are not recommended for wet areas in bathrooms.

Press sheet-vinyl flooring into fresh adhesive with a flooring roller. Rolling the vinyl creates an even surface and a solid bond. Flooring rollers are available at rental centers and flooring stores.

Everything you Need:

Tools: pry bar, hammer, marker, straightedge, circular saw, jig saw, handsaw, scissors, broom, vacuum, flooring knife, notched trowel.

Materials: plywood underlayment, tape, craft paper, ring-shank nails, flooring adhesive, vinyl flooring, finish nails, metal threshold.

Bathroom Floor Construction

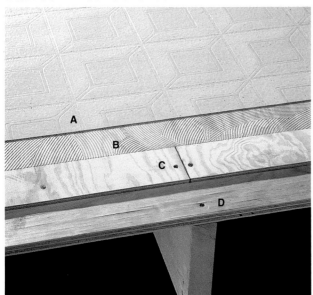

Anatomy of a sheet-vinyl floor: Sheet-vinyl flooring (A) is bonded with vinyl flooring adhesive (B) to a new underlayment of ¼"-thick, exterior-grade plywood (C). The underlayment is nailed to the subfloor (D), which can be made from plywood or diagonal floorboards. If possible, purchase sheet vinyl that is wide enough to cover the floor without a seam.

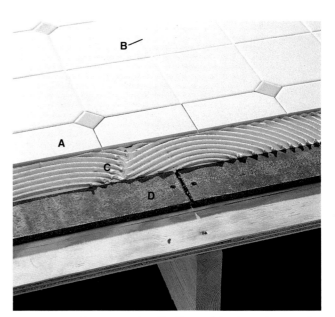

Anatomy of a ceramic tile floor: Unglazed ceramic floor tiles (A) finished with grout (B) are set into a bed of dry-set mortar (C). The mortar is applied over an underlayment of ⅝" cementboard (D). The entire floor is covered with alkaline sealer.

How to Prepare a Bathroom Floor

1 Use a flat pry bar to remove the old flooring underlayment.

2 Nail down any loose subfloor boards with ring-shank nails. Replace boards that are warped, bowed, or damaged (page 39).

3 Remove base molding, then undercut the bottom edges of door casings to make room for new underlayment and flooring. Use small pieces of underlayment and flooring as a spacing guide, then trim casings with a handsaw.

4 Lay sheets of sanded, 1/4"-thick exterior-grade plywood on the subfloor as an underlayment for sheet vinyl (use 5/8" cementboard for ceramic tile). Leave a 1/8" gap between underlayment sheets as an expansion joint.

5 Make a template of cardboard or paper for irregular areas, then trace the template outline onto the underlayment. Cut the underlayment to fit, using a jig saw.

6 Secure the underlayment with 6d ring-shank nails, driven every 8" along the edges of the plywood. Also nail down the middle of the sheets. Sweep and vacuum the surface thoroughly before installing flooring.

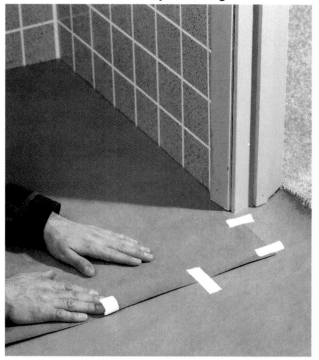

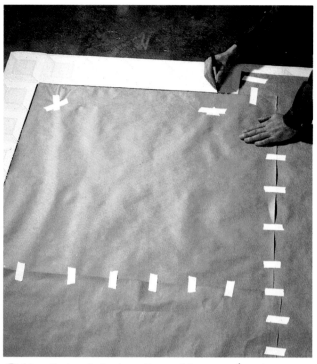

1 Make a template of the floor area by cutting sheets of heavy paper and taping them together. Make cutouts in the template for obstacles like water pipes and the toilet flange. At doorways, slide the paper under the casings.

2 Unroll sheet vinyl, pattern-side-up, on a clean, flat surface, then position the paper template over the sheet vinyl, aligning it so the edges are parallel to the pattern lines. Tape the template to the vinyl, then trace the outline onto the vinyl with a marker.

3 Remove the template, then cut the sheet vinyl along the outlines, using a sharp flooring knife and a straightedge.

4 Cut holes in vinyl for pipes and other obstacles. Slice the vinyl from the cutout to the edge, following a pattern line, so flooring can be slipped past pipes.

5 Lay flooring into position and slide the edges underneath door casings.

6 Fold back half of the flooring, then apply a layer of flooring adhesive over all of the exposed underlayment, using a ¼" notched trowel.

7 Lay the flooring back onto the adhesive, and bond the surface with a floor roller. Fold over the other half of the flooring, apply adhesive, then lay and bond the vinyl. Wipe up adhesive that oozes up around the edges of the vinyl, using a damp rag.

8 Measure and cut a strip-metal threshold to fit across the doorway, then position it over the edge of the vinyl flooring and nail it in place.

9 Install baseboard and trim moldings, using finish nails or construction adhesive. If you prefer, a neat layer of tub & tile caulk may be substituted for baseboard moldings.

Prebuilt cabinets are inexpensive and simple to install. Most manufacturers sell several cabinet types in the same style and finish. When pricing prebuilt cabinets, note that faucets and vanity tops are sold separately.

Custom-built bathroom cabinets provide unlimited design options, but they are costly.

Installing Cabinets, Countertops & Sinks

When selecting cabinets, countertops and sinks, you will need to make a choice between prebuilt cabinets and custom-made fixtures. Prebuilt cabinets and countertops are available in familiar styles at home centers, but for more unique styles you may want to have your cabinets and countertops custom-built by a professional cabinetmaker.

This section shows:

- Installing cabinets (pages 100 to 103)
- Installing countertops & sinks (pages 104 to 107)

Variations for Cabinets, Countertops & Sinks

The double vanity with an integral, two-basin countertop is a good choice for large families and for families with two working adults. The drains for many double vanities are linked together. If the vanity contains drawers between the sink basins, however, separate traps and drains are usually required.

The corner vanity and counter-top make efficient use of small spaces. Many are available with a matching corner medicine cabinet and light fixture.

The banjo countertop extends counter space, usually over a toilet located next to the sink. Most banjo countertops are custom-made from laminates, or solid-surface materials like Corian® or Swanstone®. The countertop conceals a sturdy 2 × 4 mounting frame that is attached to wall studs with lag screws.

The pedestal sink is popular in half-bathrooms where little storage is needed. The sink is screwed to the wall, and the decorative pedestal is bolted to the floor.

Remove the doors and drawers on heavy cabinets before installing them to make them easier to move and to give yourself better access for making plumbing hookups. Reattach the doors and install drawers after the plumbing hookups are completed.

Installing Cabinets

Common bathroom cabinets include vanities, medicine cabinets, linen cabinets, and "tank topper" cabinets that mount over the toilet area.

When installing cabinets in damp locations, like a bathroom, choose the best cabinets you can afford. Look for quality indicators, like doweled construction, hardwood doors and drawers, and high-gloss, moisture-resistant finishes. Avoid cabinets with sides or doors that are painted on one side, and finished with laminate or veneer on the other, because these cabinets are more likely to warp.

Everything You Need:

Tools: electronic stud finder, marker, level, pry bar, hammer, cordless screwdriver, drill, circular saw, reciprocating saw, bar clamp, carpenter's square, protective equipment.

Materials: duplex nails, 10d common nails, finish nails, 1 × 4 board, 2¹/₂" wood screws, wood shims.

How to Install a Surface-mounted Cabinet

1 Locate wall studs and mark them clearly on the wall surface. Draw a level line at the desired top height of the cabinet body, then measure and mark a second line to indicate the bottom of the cabinet.

2 Attach a temporary ledger board (usually 1 × 4) just below the lower level line, using duplex nails. Nail holes can be patched with wallboard compound after the cabinet installation is completed.

3 Rest the base of the cabinet on the ledger, and hold it in place, or brace it with 2 × 4s. Attach the cabinet to the wall at stud locations by drilling pilot holes and driving wood screws. Remove ledger when finished.

How to Install a Recessed Cabinet

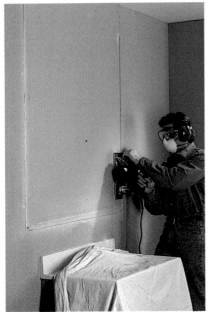

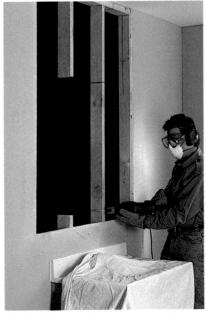

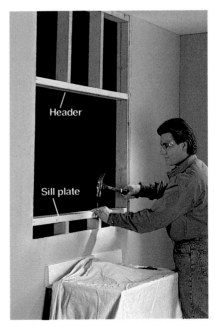

1 Locate the first stud beyond either side of planned cabinet location, then remove wall surface between these studs. (Removing wall surface all the way to the ceiling simplifies patching work.) Cut along the center of studs, using a circular saw with blade depth set to equal thickness of wall surface.

2 Mark a rough opening ½" taller than cabinet frame onto the exposed wall studs. Add 1½" for each header and sill plate, then cut out studs in rough opening area (see page 14 before cutting wall studs).

3 Frame out the top and bottom of the rough opening by installing a header and a sill plate between the cut wall studs. Make sure the header and sill plate are level, then nail them in place with 10d common nails.

4 Mark the rough opening width on the header and sill plates, centering the opening over the sink. Cut and nail jack studs between the header and the sill plate, just outside the rough opening marks. NOTE: Do any wiring work for light fixtures (pages 52 to 55), then install new wall surface (pages 82 to 83) before proceeding.

5 Position the cabinet in the opening. Check it for level with a carpenter's level, then attach the cabinet by drilling pilot holes and driving wood screws through the top and bottom of the cabinet sides and into the wall studs, header, and sill plate. Attach doors, shelves, and hardware.

How to Install a Vanity

1 Mark the top edge of the vanity cabinet on the wall. Using a carpenter's level, draw a level line at the cabinet height.

2 Slide the vanity into position. The back of the cabinet should be flush against the wall. (If the wall surface is uneven, position the vanity so it contacts the wall in at least one spot, and the back cabinet rail is parallel with the wall.)

3 Shim below the vanity until it is level, using the line on the wall as a guide.

Two or more cabinets: Set the cabinets in position against the wall, and align the cabinet fronts. If one cabinet is higher than the other, shim under the lower cabinet until the two cabinets are even. Clamp the cabinet faces together, then drill countersunk pilot holes through the face frames, spaced 12" apart, at least halfway into the face frame of the second cabinet. Drive wood screws through the pilot holes to join the cabinets together.

4 Locate wall studs, then drive 2½" wallboard screws through the rail on the cabinet back and into wall studs. Screws should be driven at both corners and in the center of the back rail.

5 Attach any trim and molding required to cover the gaps between the vanity and the wall, and between the vanity and the floor. (Small gaps may be filled with caulk instead.) See pages 104 to 106 for instructions on installing sinks and countertops.

Variations for Vanity Installations

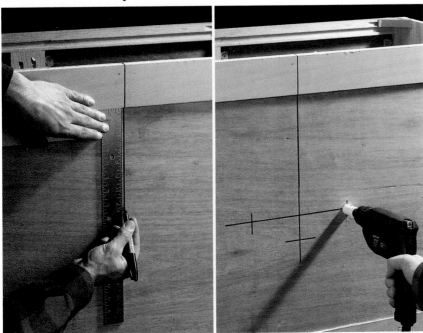

Vanities with backs: Mark a line on the wall where the top of vanity will fit, then draw a line down the wall from the midpoint of this line. Draw a corresponding center line down the back of the vanity. Measure the distance from the supply and drain pipes to the center line on the wall. Transfer distances to the back of the vanity, measuring from the center line. Mark pipe cutouts, then cut with a hole saw or a jig saw.

Raise a vanity to a more convenient height by attaching an extension made of 2 × 4s to the base of the vanity. Attach the extension by screwing through the cabinet sides and into the 2 × 4s.

Installing Countertops & Sinks

Most bathroom countertops installed today are integral (one-piece) sink-countertop units made from cultured marble or other solid materials, like Corian® or Swanstone®. Integral sink-countertops are convenient, and many are inexpensive, but style and color options are limited.

Some remodelers and designers still prefer the distinctive look of a custom-built countertop with a self-rimming sink basin, which gives you a much greater selection of styles and colors. Installing a self-rimming sink is very simple.

Integral sink-countertops are made in standard sizes to fit common vanity widths. Because the sink and countertop are cast from the same material, integral sink-countertops do not leak, and do not require extensive caulking and sealing.

Everything You Need:

Tools: pencil, scissors, carpenter's level, screwdriver, channel-type pliers, ratchet wrench, basin wrench.

Materials: cardboard, plumber's putty, lag screws, tub & tile caulk.

Options for Vanity Countertops

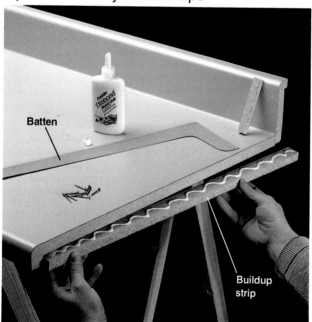

Postform countertops are made from inexpensive, factory-laminated particle board, usually with a built-in backsplash and front flange. Buildup strips and battens are used to finish the edges of the countertops, and holes for the sink basins are cut to size using a jig saw. Countertops are held in place with corner braces (page opposite) and caulk.

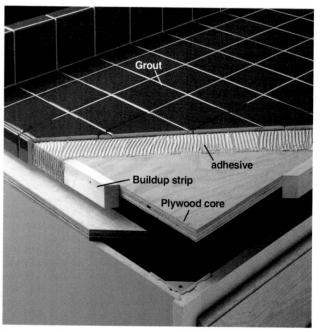

Ceramic tile countertops are made with sanded ¾" plywood and 1 × 2 buildup strips, and finished with a ceramic tile surface (see pages 86 to 93). To save time and tile, cut out the sink hole before laying tile.

How to Install an Integral Sink-Countertop

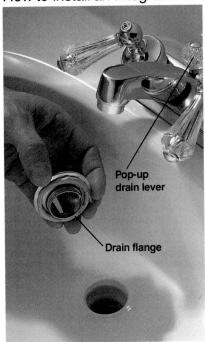

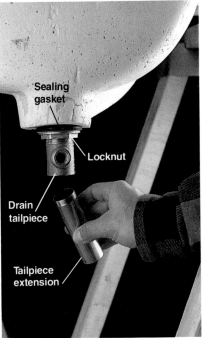

Pop-up drain lever

Drain flange

Sealing gasket

Locknut

Drain tailpiece

Tailpiece extension

1 Set sink-countertop onto saw-horses. Attach faucet (page 111), and slip the drain lever through the faucet body. Place a ring of plumber's putty around the drain flange, then insert the flange in the drain opening.

2 Thread locknut and sealing gasket onto drain tailpiece, then insert tailpiece into drain opening and screw it onto drain flange. Tighten locknut securely. Attach tailpiece extension. Insert pop-up stopper linkage (page 28).

3 Apply a layer of tub & tile caulk (or adhesive if specified by the countertop manufacturer) to the top edges of the vanity, and to any corner braces.

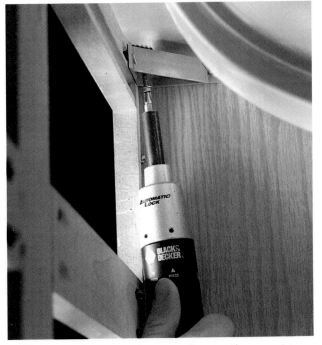

4 Center the sink-countertop unit over the vanity, so the overhang is equal on both sides and the backsplash of the countertop is flush with the wall. Press the countertop evenly into the caulk.

Cabinets with corner braces: Secure the counter-top to the cabinet by driving a mounting screw through each corner brace and up into the counter-top. Cultured marble and other hard countertops require predrilling and a plastic screw sleeve.

(continued next page)

How to Install an Integral Sink-Countertop (continued)

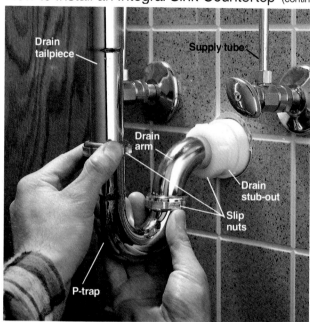

5 Attach the drain arm to the drain stub-out, using a slip nut. Attach one end of the P-trap to the drain arm, and the other to the tailpiece of the sink drain, using slip nuts. Connect supply tubes to the faucet tailpieces (page 111).

6 Seal the gap between the backsplash and the wall with tub & tile caulk (page 124).

How to Install a Drop-in Sink

1 Use a template that is ½" narrower than the sink rim to mark the countertop cutout. Drill a ⅜" starter hole, then use a jig saw to make the cutout. For countertop-mounted faucets, drill faucet tailpiece holes according to faucet manufacturer's directions.

2 Apply a ring of plumber's putty around the sink cutout. Before setting the sink in place, attach the faucet body to the sink or countertop (page 111), then attach the drainpiece and drain flange (page 105, step 1) and the pop-up drain assembly.

3 Set the sink into the cutout area, and gently press the rim of the sink into the plumber's putty. Hook up the drain and supply fittings (step 5, above), then caulk around the sink rim.

How to Install a Pedestal Sink

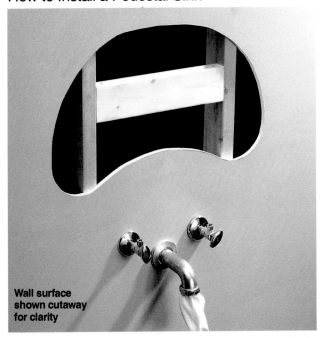

1 Install 2 × 4 blocking between wall studs, behind the planned sink location. Cover the wall with water-resistant wallboard (pages 82 to 83).

2 Set the basin and pedestal in position, bracing the basin with 2 × 4s. Outline the top of the basin on the wall, and mark the base of the pedestal on the floor. Mark reference points on the wall and floor through the mounting holes found on the back of the sink and the bottom of the pedestal.

3 Set aside the basin and pedestal. Drill pilot holes in the wall and floor at reference points, then reposition the pedestal. Anchor the pedestal to the floor with lag screws.

4 Attach the faucet (page 111), then set the sink on the pedestal. Align the holes in the back of the sink with the pilot holes drilled in the wall, then drive lag screws and washers into the wall brace, using a ratchet wrench. Do not overtighten.

5 Hook up the drain and supply fittings (see pages 106 and 111). Caulk between the back of the sink and the wall when installation is finished (page 124).

107

Completing a Bathroom Remodeling Project

Careful, accurate finishing work helps ensure that all the parts of your bathroom remodeling project function properly and look good.

Shop carefully when purchasing faucets and electrical fixtures. With these products, spending a few dollars more for better quality is always a good investment.

Be extra careful when working with wiring in a bathroom, where the closeness of water poses a constant threat. Always turn off electrical power at the main service panel before you begin an electrical project.

Take special precautions to avoid damaging faucets and accessories that have a polished finish. Wrap the jaws of pliers with masking tape before tightening visible nuts, and use care when driving screws so the screwdriver does not slip and cause damage. Block drain openings to avoid losing small pieces of hardware in sinks and bathtubs.

This section shows:

- Installing faucets & spouts (pages 109 to 111)
- Installing a toilet (pages 112 to 113)
- Installing electrical fixtures (pages 114 to 115)
- Installing a vent fan (pages 116 to 119)
- Installing accessories (pages 120 to 123)
- Waterproofing and maintenance (pages 124 to 125)

Installing Faucets & Spouts

One-piece faucets, with either one or two handles, are the most popular fixtures for bathroom installations. "Widespread" faucets with separate spout and handles are being installed with increasing frequency, however. Because the handles are connected to the spout with flex tubes that can be 18" or longer, widespread faucets can be arranged in many ways.

Everything You Need:

Tools: drill with spade bit, basin wrench, adjustable wrench, screwdriver.

Materials: plumber's putty, Teflon® tape, joint compound.

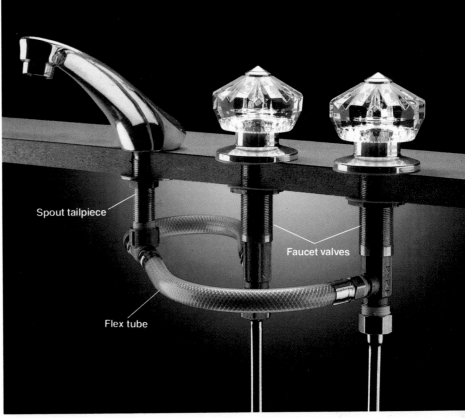

Spout tailpiece

Faucet valves

Flex tube

Widespread faucets have handles that are installed separately from the spout. Installed most often with whirlpools, widespread faucets also are becoming popular for sinks. The possibilities for arranging widespread faucets are limited only by the length of the flex tubes that connect the faucet handle valves to the spout.

How to Connect Supply Tubes & Spouts

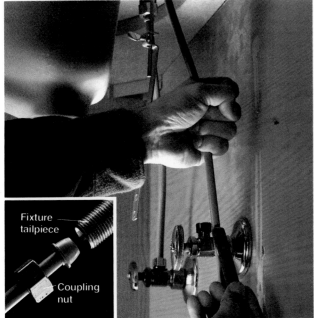

Fixture tailpiece

Coupling nut

Connect supply tubes after the sink and faucet body are installed. Tubes should be slightly longer than the distance from the shutoff valves to the faucet tailpieces. Most tubes have a flared end that fits into the faucet tailpiece (inset). Wrap threads of tailpieces with Teflon® tape before attaching tubes.

Connect tub spouts by applying joint compound or Teflon® tape to the threaded end of the spout nipple that extends from the wall (left). Screw the spout onto the nipple, using a long screwdriver as a lever (right). Some spouts have a set screw on the underside that must be tightened.

How to Install a Widespread Faucet

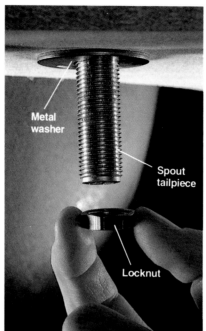

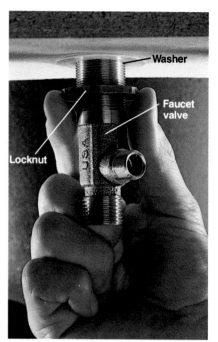

1 Drill holes for faucet handles and spout in deck or countertop, according to manufacturer's suggestions. Slide a protective washer onto the spout tailpiece, then insert the tailpiece into the spout hole.

2 From beneath the deck, slide a metal washer onto spout tailpiece, then attach a locknut. Tighten the nut by hand, then check to make sure the spout is properly aligned. Tighten with a basin wrench until snug.

3 Attach faucet valves to deck, using washers and locknuts, as directed by the manufacturer. NOTE: Some widespread faucet valves, like the one above, are inserted up through the hole, and have locknuts above and below.

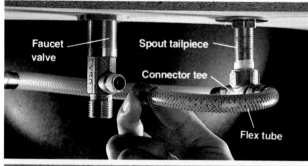

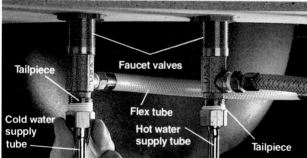

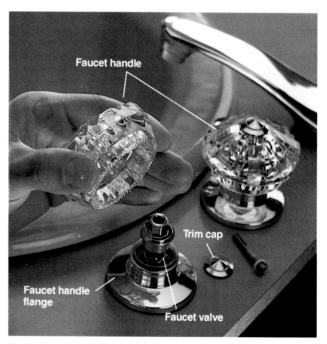

4 Wrap Teflon® tape around spout tailpiece, then attach the connector tee to the tailpiece. Attach one end of each flex tube to the tee, and the other end to the proper faucet valve (top). Wrap Teflon® tape around faucet valve tailpieces, then attach hot and cold water supply tubes to tailpieces (bottom).

5 Attach faucet handle flanges and faucet handles, according to manufacturer's directions. Cover exposed screw heads with trim caps. (See pages 105 to 106 for drain hookup information.)

How to Install a One-piece Faucet

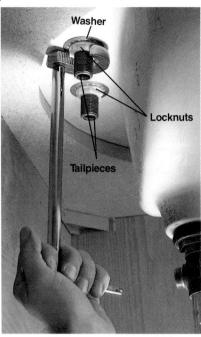

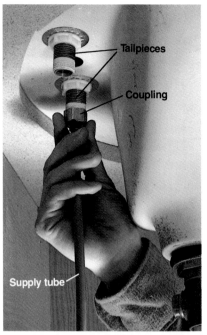

1 Apply a ring of plumber's putty around the base of the faucet body. (Some faucets use a gasket that does not require plumber's putty—read the manufacturer's directions carefully.)

2 Insert the faucet tailpieces through holes in countertop or sink. From below, thread washers and locknuts over the tailpieces, then tighten the locknuts with a basin wrench until snug.

3 Wrap Teflon® tape around the tailpiece threads, then attach the supply tube couplings and tighten until snug. Connect drain linkage (pages 105 to 106), then attach handles and trim caps.

How to Install Tub & Shower Faucets

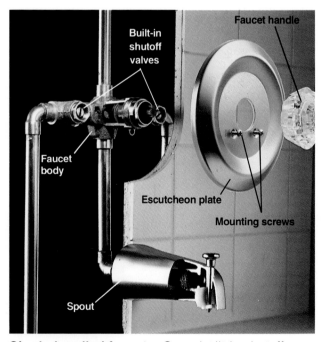

Two-handled faucet: Screw handle flanges onto faucet valve stems, then attach handles to stems, using mounting screws. Attach spout (page 109) and trim caps. NOTE: Faucet body is attached before wall surface is installed (page 64).

Single-handled faucets: Open built-in shutoff valves, using a screwdriver, then attach escutcheon plate to faucet body with mounting screws. Attach faucet handle with mounting screw, then attach spout (page 109) and trim cap. NOTE: Faucet body is attached before wall surface is installed (page 64).

Installing Toilets

Most toilets in the low-to-moderate price range are two-piece units, with a separate tank and bowl, made of vitreous china. One-piece toilets, with integral tank and bowl, also are available, but the cost is usually two or three times that of two-piece units.

Standard toilets have 3.5-gallon tanks, but water-saver toilets, with 1.6-gallon tanks, are becoming increasingly common. A few states now require water-saver toilets in new construction.

Install a toilet by anchoring the bowl to the floor first, then mounting the tank onto the bowl. China fixtures crack easily, so use care when handling them.

Everything You Need:

Tools: adjustable wrench, ratchet wrench or basin wrench, screwdriver.

Materials: wax ring & sleeve, plumber's putty, floor bolts, tank bolts with rubber washers, seat bolts and mounting nuts.

How to Install a Toilet

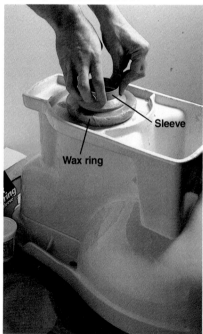

1 Turn the bowl upside down, and place a new wax ring and sleeve onto the toilet horn. Apply a ring of plumber's putty around the bottom edge of the toilet base.

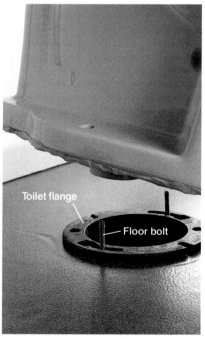

2 Position the toilet over the toilet flange so the floor bolts fit through the holes in the base of the toilet. The flange should be clean, and the floor bolts should point straight up.

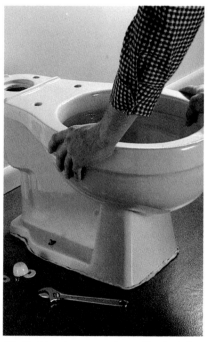

3 Press down on the toilet bowl to compress the wax ring and plumber's putty. Attach washers and nuts to the floor bolts, and tighten with an adjustable wrench until snug. Do not overtighten. Attach trim caps.

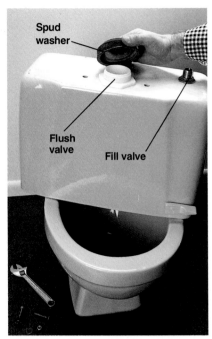

4 Turn the tank upside down, and set the spud washer over the tailpiece of the flush valve. Turn tank right-side up. NOTE: with some toilets, you will need to purchase a flush handle, fill valve, and flush valve separately.

5 Set the tank onto the bowl, centering the spud washer over the water inlet opening near the back edge of the bowl.

6 Shift the tank gently until the tank bolt holes in the tank are aligned over the tank bolt holes in the bowl flange. Place rubber washers onto tank bolts, then insert the bolts down through the holes in the tank.

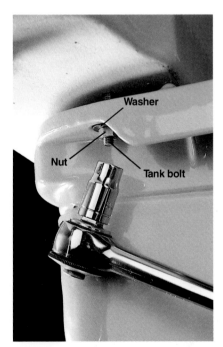

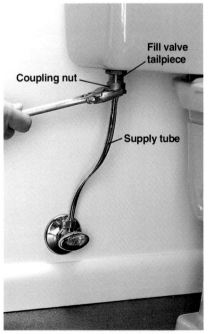

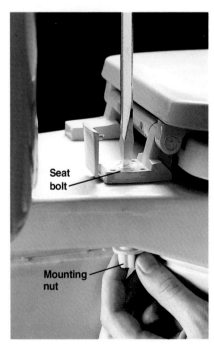

7 From beneath the bowl flange, attach washers and nuts to the tank bolts, and tighten with a ratchet wrench or basin wrench until snug. Do not overtighten.

8 Cut a piece of supply tube to fit between the shutoff valve and the toilet tank. Attach the tube to the shutoff valve, then to the fill valve tailpiece. Use an adjustable wrench to tighten coupling nuts until they are snug.

9 Mount the toilet seat onto the bowl by tightening the mounting nuts onto the seat bolts from below the seat flange.

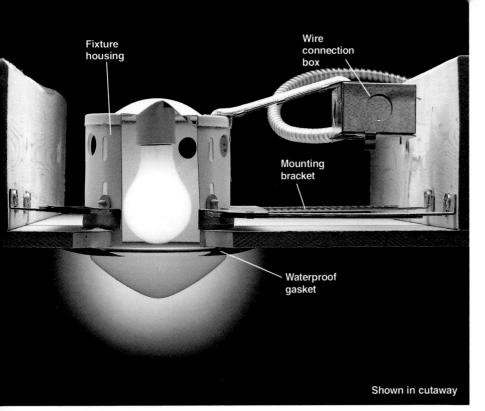

Fixture housing

Wire connection box

Mounting bracket

Waterproof gasket

Shown in cutaway

Installing Electrical Fixtures

Running cables for new electrical fixtures is easiest if wall surfaces have been removed (pages 38 to 40). Make the final wiring hookups at the fixtures after wall surfaces are finished (pages 82 to 83).

Follow Local Code requirements for wiring bathrooms. Reduce shock hazard by protecting the entire bathroom circuit with GFCI receptacles. Install only electrical fixtures that are U.L.-approved.

If it is not practical to remove wall surfaces, "retrofit" techniques can be used to install vent fans and other fixtures (pages 52 to 55). Most wiring connections for bathroom fixtures are easy to make, but wiring configurations in electrical boxes vary widely, depending on the type of fixture and the circuit layout.

If you are not confident in your skills, have an electrician install and connect fixtures. Unless you are very experienced, leave the job of making circuit connections at the main service panel to an electrician.

Installing most bathroom lights is similar to installing lights in any other room in the house. Adding new lighting fixtures makes a bathroom safer and more inviting, and can even make bathrooms seem larger. In showers, install only vaporproof lights, like the one above, that have been U.L. rated for wet areas. Shower lights have a waterproof gasket that fits between the fixture and the light cover.

CAUTION: Always shut off electrical power at the main service panel, and test for power (page 37) before working with wires.

Everything You Need:

Tools: neon circuit tester, wire stripper, cable ripper, screwdriver, level.

Materials: NM cable, wire staples, wire nuts, screws.

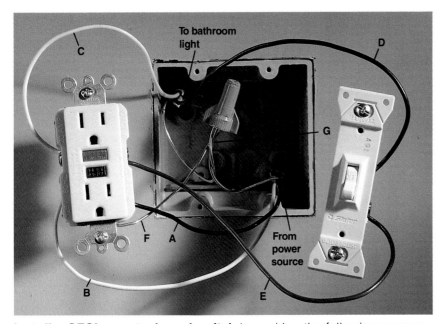

To bathroom light

C

D

G

From power source

F   A

B   E

Install a GFCI receptacle and switch by making the following connections: black wire from power source (A) to brass screw marked LINE on GFCI; white wire from power source (B) to silver screw marked LINE; white wire to light (C) to silver GFCI screw marked LOAD; black wire to light (D) to a screw terminal on switch. Cut a short length of black wire (E), and attach one end to brass GFCI screw marked LOAD, and other end to a screw terminal on switch. Connect a bare grounding pigtail wire to GFCI grounding screw (F), and join all bare grounding wires (G) with a wire nut. Tuck wires into box, then attach switch, receptacle, and coverplate. See page 53 for circuit diagram.

How to Install a Bathroom Light Fixture

1 Turn power off. Remove coverplate from light fixture, and feed the electrical cable through the hole in the back of the fixture. NOTE: Some bathroom lights, like the shower light on page 114, have a connection box that is separate from the light fixture.

2 Position the fixture in the planned location, and adjust it so it is level. (Center the fixture if it is being installed over a medicine cabinet.) If possible, attach the box at wall stud locations. If studs are not conveniently located, anchor the box to the wall, using toggle bolts or other connectors (page 120).

3 Make electrical connections: attach white wire from cable (A) to white fixture wire (B), using a wire nut; attach black wire from cable (C) to black fixture wire (D); connect bare copper grounding wire from cable (E) to the fixture grounding wire (F) (or attach to grounding screw in some fixtures).

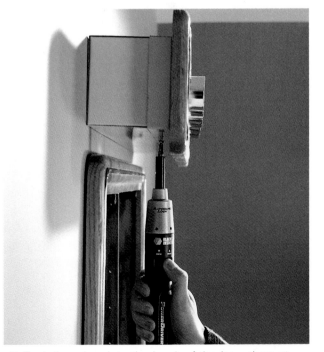

4 Tuck the wires into the back of the box, then attach the fixture coverplate. Install unprotected light bulbs only after the rest of the remodeling project is completed.

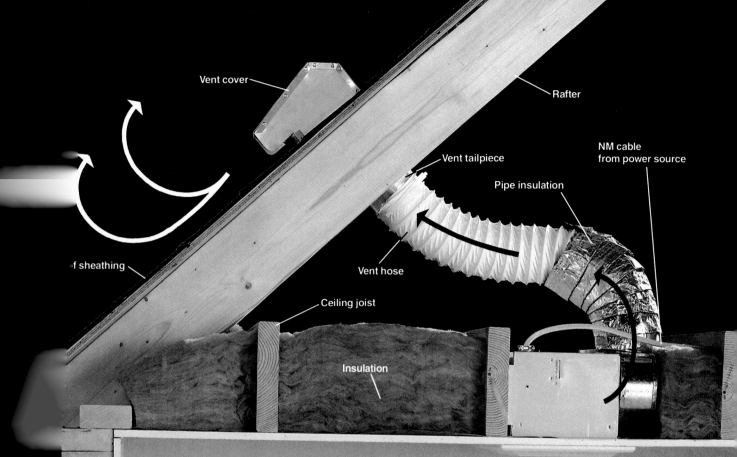

Vent cover

Rafter

Vent tailpiece

NM cable
from power source

Pipe insulation

f sheathing

Vent hose

Ceiling joist

Insulation

Installing a Vent Fan

A vent fan makes your bathroom safer and more comfortable by removing heat, moisture, and odors. Building Codes usually require that all bathrooms without natural ventilation be equipped with a vent fan, but even if your bathroom has a window or skylight, installing a vent fan is a good idea.

Vent fans with only a light fixture usually may be wired into your main bathroom electrical circuit, but units with built-in heat lamps or heat blowers require a separate electrical circuit.

Most vent fans are installed in the center of the bathroom ceiling, or over the toilet area. Do not install a vent fan unit over the tub or shower area unless it is GFCI-protected and rated for use in wet areas.

If the vent fan you choose does not come with a complete mounting kit, purchase one separately. Vent fan mounting kits should include: vent hose, vent tailpiece, and exterior vent cover.

Vent fans may be installed while wall surfaces are removed, or as a retrofit.

Fan rating
(cubic feet
per minute)

70 — C.F.M.
AT .10 WG
4.0 — SONE rating

C-K3285 SONES

Check the information label attached to each vent fan unit. Choose a unit with a **fan rating** at least 5 CFM higher than the square footage of your bathroom. **SONES** refer to the relative quietness of the unit, rated on a scale of 1 to 7. (Quieter vant fans have lower SONE ratings.)

Everything You Need:

Tools: pencil, drill, jig saw, hammer, screwdrivers, caulk gun, reciprocating saw, wire stripper, pliers.

Materials: wallboard screws, 2" dimension lumber, NM cable (14-2, 14-3), wire nuts, electrical box, hose clamps, pipe insulation, switches, roofing cement, self-sealing roofing nails.

How to Install a Vent Fan

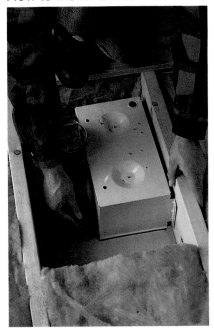

1 Position the vent fan unit against a ceiling joist. Outline the vent fan onto the ceiling, from above. Remove unit, then drill pilot holes at the corners of the outline and cut out the area with a jig saw or wallboard saw.

2 Remove the grille from the fan box, then position box against a joist, with the edge recessed 1/4" from the finished surface of the ceiling (so the grille can be flush-mounted). Attach box to joist, using wallboard screws.

Vent fans with heaters or light fixtures: Some manufacturers recommend using 2" dimension lumber to build dams between the ceiling joists to keep insulation at least 6" away from the vent fan unit.

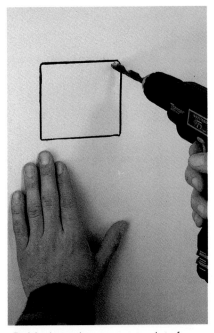

3 Mark and cut an opening for the switch box on the wall next to the latch side of the bathroom door, then run a 14-gauge, 3-wire NM cable from the switch cutout to the vent fan unit (see page 54).

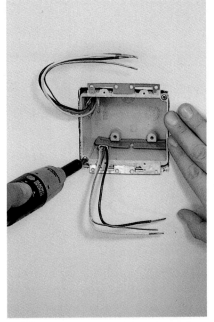

4 Strip 10" of sheathing from the end of the cable, then feed cable into switch box so at least 1/2" of sheathing extends into the box. Tighten mounting screws until box is secure.

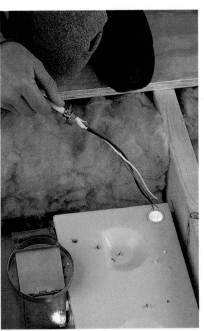

5 Strip 10" of sheathing from the end of the cable at the vent box, then attach the cable to a cable clamp. Insert the cable into the fan box. From inside of box, screw a locknut onto the threaded end of the clamp.

(continued next page)

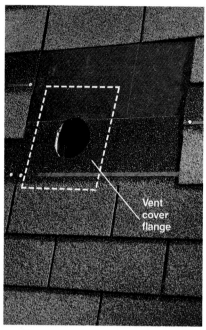

Vent cover flange

6 Mark the exit location in the roof for the vent hose, next to a rafter. Drill a pilot hole, then saw through the sheathing and roofing material with a reciprocating saw to make the cutout for the vent tailpiece.

7 From outside, remove section of shingles from around the cutout, leaving roofing paper intact. Removed shingles should create an exposed area the size of the vent cover flange. Use caution when working on a roof.

8 Attach a hose clamp to the rafter next to the roof cutout, about 1" below the roof sheathing (top photo). Insert the vent tailpiece into the cutout and through the hose clamp, then tighten the clamp screw (bottom photo).

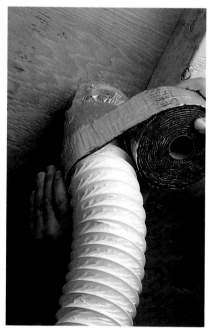

9 Slide one end of vent hose over the tailpiece, and slide the other end over the outlet on the fan unit. Slip hose clamps or straps around each end of the vent hose, and tighten to secure hose in place.

10 Wrap the vent hose with pipe insulation. Insulation prevents moist air inside the hose from condensing and dripping down into the fan motor.

11 Apply roofing cement to the bottom of the vent cover flange, then slide the vent cover over the tailpiece. Nail the vent cover flange in place with self-sealing roofing nails, then patch in shingles around cover.

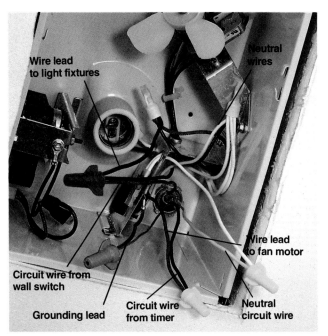

Wire lead to light fixtures

Neutral wires

Wire lead to fan motor

Circuit wire from wall switch

Grounding lead

Circuit wire from timer

Neutral circuit wire

12 Make the following wire connections at the fan box: black circuit wire from timer to wire lead for fan motor; red circuit wire from single-pole switch to wire lead for light fixtures; white neutral circuit wire to neutral wire lead; circuit grounding wire to grounding lead in fan box. Attach coverplate over box when wiring is completed.

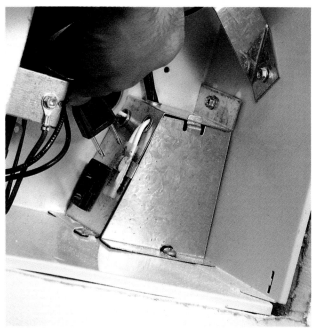

13 Connect the fan motor plug to the built-in receptacle on the wire connection box, and attach the fan grille to the frame, using the mounting clips included with the fan kit. NOTE: If wall and ceiling surfaces have been removed for installation, install new surfaces before completing this step.

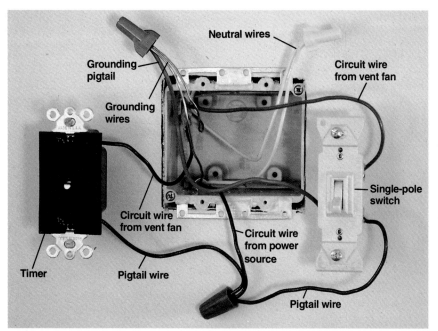

Grounding pigtail

Neutral wires

Circuit wire from vent fan

Grounding wires

Single-pole switch

Circuit wire from vent fan

Circuit wire from power source

Timer

Pigtail wire

Pigtail wire

14 At wall switch box, add black pigtail wires to one screw terminal on the timer and to one screw terminal on the single-pole switch; add a green grounding pigtail to grounding screw on single-pole switch. Make following wire connections: black circuit wire from power source to black pigtail wires; black circuit wire from vent fan to remaining screw on timer; red circuit wire from vent fan to remaining screw on single-pole switch. Join white wires with a wire nut. Join grounding wires with a green wire nut.

15 Tuck the wires into the wall switch box, then attach the switches to the box and attach coverplates and timer dial. Turn on the power.

Fill bathtubs and whirlpools at least half full of water before caulking around the edges to approximate the full tub weight. Tubs shift position when filled with water; caulking when the tub is full helps ensure that the caulking seal does not stretch and pull apart when the tub is filled.

Options for Attaching Bathroom Accessories

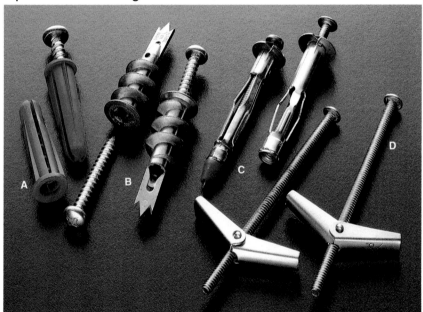

Attach accessories and hardware between wall studs by using screw sleeves or special fasteners that are attached directly to the wall surface. Plastic anchor sleeves (A), often used in ceramic tile, are inserted into pilot holes, where they expand when screws are driven. Grip-it® fasteners (B), molly bolts (C), and toggle bolts (D) provide more holding power than sleeves.

Making Finishing Touches

Hanging towel rods, mirrors, and other accessories, caulking seams, and sealing tile and grout are a few of the small projects that bring your bathroom remodeling project to completion.

Whenever possible, anchor accessories to wall studs or blocking for maximum holding power. If no studs or blocking are located in the area where accessories will be installed, use special fasteners, like toggle bolts or molly bolts, to anchor the accessories to wallboard or plaster walls.

Use tub & tile caulk for most bathroom sealing projects. Most tub & tile caulk is a blend of silicone and latex that offers the best features of both. Pure silicone expands and contracts with fixtures, like bathtubs, that can shift position. It is a long-lasting, effective sealant, but it is relatively expensive and cannot be painted.

Latex caulk is inexpensive and it holds paint well. It also is easy to apply in smooth, neat beads, but it breaks down more quickly than silicone, and it can trap odors and mildew. Some tub & tile caulk contains acrylic for a hard surface. Caulk of all types should be inspected yearly, and reapplied as needed.

Everything You Need:

Tools: tape measure, jig saw with metal-cutting blade or hacksaw, drill, caulk gun, grout float.

Materials: caulk, screws, sleeves and anchors, tape.

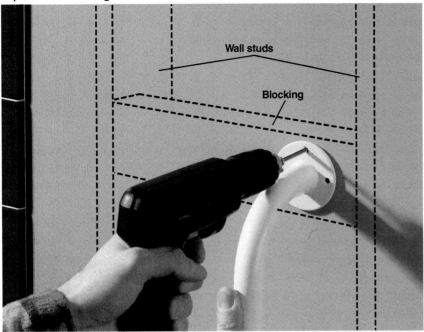

Install safety grab bars only over wall studs or blocking so they do not tear loose from the wall when they are used. Blocking is easiest to install when wall surfaces are fully removed (pages 38 to 40). The alternative is to cut out a small section of wall surface between studs, install blocking, then patch the wall surface.

Apply a dab of silicone caulk over pilot holes and screw tips before inserting screws in or near high-moisture areas. Caulk keeps moisture out of walls and enhances the holding power of screws.

Select bathroom accessories that fit onto a metal mounting plate, which can be firmly anchored to the wall. Commonly used with porcelain bathroom accessories, mounting plates are hidden from view once the installation is completed.

Apply a bead of caulk to the back of the mounting flange on recessed wall accessories to keep moisture out and prevent the accessory from shifting. Recessed accessories fit into cutouts in the wall surface and are attached to wall framing members or blocking. If possible, install blocking while wall surfaces are removed.

How to Install a Shower Door

1 Measure the length of the shower curb to make sure the shower door will fit, and to find the required length of the shower door threshold.

2 Cut the shower door threshold to the correct length, using a jig saw with a metal cutting blade, or a hacksaw.

3 Apply a heavy bead of silicone caulk to the underside of the threshold, then position it on the curb. Never attach a shower door threshold with screws or other fasteners that can puncture the shower curb.

Jamb shown cutaway for clarity

4 Attach the side jambs to the shower stall frame as directed by the shower door manufacturer.

Threshold screw

Pin opening

Hinge pin

Adjustable side jamb

5 Adjust the side jamb so the door opening is the right size for the shower door, then lock the jamb in position (most doors have a threshold screw that secures the adjustable jamb). Slip the hinge pins into the pin openings (inset).

6 Measure opening and cut the top jamb, then screw it to the side jambs. Attach door handles and any waterproofing hardware or trim. Caulk all joints thoroughly (page 124).

Options for Installing Shower Curtain Rods

Telescoping shower curtain rod: Spring-loaded and telescoping shower curtain rods are quick and easy to install. They are less sturdy than permanent shower rods, but they will not damage your shower stall or bathtub surround.

Permanent shower curtain rod: Mounting brackets that hold shower curtain rods in place are strong, especially if attached to framing members. Screws for brackets will puncture walls, so caulk generously around brackets.

How to Install a Bathroom Mirror

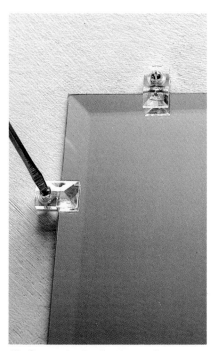

1 Using a pencil, draw a level line at the planned height of the mirror, then hold the mirror top against the level line, and outline all mirror corners.

2 Using corner marks as a reference, mark the location of screws for mirror clips (two per corner). Drill a pilot hole, then drive a plastic screw anchor at each mark. using a hammer.

3 Screw in the bottom mirror clips, then set the mirror on bottom clips and attach remaining clips on the sides and top of mirror. Have a helper support heavier mirrors while you work.

How to Apply Tub & Tile Caulk

1 Clean the surface thoroughly, using warm soapy water and a sponge or toothbrush.

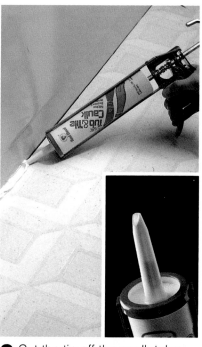

2 Cut the tip off the caulk tube at a slanted angle, then snip off the point to provide a flat application surface (inset). Apply a smooth bead of caulk to the seam.

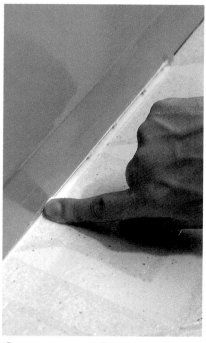

3 Moisten one of your fingers and run it along the caulk bead to smooth out any rough or uneven areas.

Tips for Bathroom Tile Maintenance

Apply sealer to grout and unglazed floor tile. Alkaline-based sealer is recommended by most tile manufacturers because it does not scrape off or scuff as quickly as silicone sealer or acrylic floor polish. Sealer should be reapplied every year.

Replace broken tiles: Break old tile into small pieces with a hammer and chisel, then scrape off the debris and old grout with a sharp paint scraper. Clean the wall surface, then apply adhesive to the back of the new tile and twist into place. Let adhesive dry for 24 hours, then apply grout (page 125).

How to Regrout Ceramic Tile

1 Scrape out the old grout with an awl, utility knife or grout tool to create a clean bed for the new grout. Old ceramic tile grout needs to be replaced every few years—and more frequently in shower stalls and other high-moisture areas. Remove and replace any broken tiles (page 124).

2 Clean the grout joints with warm soapy water and a sponge, then rinse and allow joints to dry.

3 Use a grout float to spread premixed, mildew-resistant grout over the entire tile surface. Work the grout into the joints, then let it set until it is firm. Carefully wipe away any excess grout, using a damp sponge or cloth.

4 Let the grout dry overnight, then wipe away the powdery residue with a dry, soft cloth, and coat with grout sealer. Do not expose grout to moisture for at least 24 hours.

INDEX

For Product Information:

If you have difficulty finding any of
the following materials featured in
this book, call the manufacturers
and ask for the name of the nearest
sales representatives. The representatives can direct you to local
retailers that stock these useful
products.

Bathroom cabinets (pages 98- 101)
General Marble Co. (Vanity Flair®)
   telephone: 1-800-854-7957

Bathroom fixtures
Kohler Inc.
   telephone: 1-800-4KOHLER x716

Ceramic tile (pages 80-93)
American Olean
   telephone: 1-215-393-2237

General information
National Kitchen & Bath Association
   telephone: 1-908-852-0033

**Shower surrounds, tileboard
(pages 66-67, 84-85)**
Trayco Inc.
   telephone: 1-313-664-8501

**Faucets and fittings
(pages 109-111)**
Price-Pfister Inc.
   telephone: 1-818-896-1141

**Vent fans and accessories
(pages 116-119)**
NuTone
   telephone: 1-800-543-8687

Vinyl flooring (pages 94-97)
Armstrong World Industries
   telephone: 1-800-233-3823

Whirlpool tubs (pages 74-79)
Pearl Baths Inc.
   telephone: 1-800-328-2531

Cy DeCosse Incorporated offers a variety
of how-to books. For information write:
   Cy DeCosse Subscriber Books
   5900 Green Oak Drive
   Minnetonka, MN 55343